LIVE AND LEAD LIKE A GORILLA

HOW TO LIVE AND LEAD WITH STRENGTH, COMPASSION, AND WISDOM

BRIAN EDWARDS

Copyright © 2024 by Brian Edwards
All rights reserved.

No part of this book may be reproduced, distributed, or transmitted in any form or by any means, including photocopying, recording, or other electronic or mechanical methods, without the prior written permission of the publisher, except in the case of brief quotations embodied in critical reviews and certain other noncommercial uses permitted by copyright law.

ISBN: 9798301022999

This book is a work of nonfiction. Any references to real people, living or dead, are entirely coincidental and unintentional.

Published by The Vanilla Gorilla
Raleigh, NC 2024

Printed in the United States of America

DEDICATION

To Ethan, my son and my best friend,

From the moment you entered my life, you brought with you a light that illuminated every corner of my world. You were more than my son—you were my companion, my partner in every project, my source of laughter and joy. With you, the ordinary became extraordinary. Whether we were building a hovercraft, hiking in the woods, working on a science fair project, or simply sharing time together, you transformed each day into an adventure, a chance to connect and discover.

Ethan, you were brilliant—not only in mind but in spirit. Your heart was vast and generous, and you moved through life with a warmth and kindness that made everyone around you feel valued. As I watched you grow, I saw a young man of intelligence and capability but also of compassion, someone who engaged with life with a curiosity and openness that was years beyond your age. Your boundless energy, your eagerness to learn, and your kindness touched everyone you met. You radiated a light that shone effortlessly and brightly, a light that, though far too brief, left an indelible mark on this world.

Your potential was limitless, and every challenge we tackled side by side reminded me of that. You approached life with an inquisitive mind and a profound empathy that created space for others to be themselves. Though you never sought the spotlight, you were always at the center, radiating a warmth that drew people in. That light, Ethan, remains with me, a reminder of the love and joy you shared.

Losing you changed me profoundly. It broke me open, leaving me uncertain of how to go forward in a world without you. For a long time, I was adrift. But through that pain, I came to realize that you are still with me, in every step I take and in every lesson you taught. You showed me that love is not just a feeling but an effort, a presence, and an appreciation of those we hold dear.

In losing you, I learned anew the meaning of family and friendship. Your absence taught me to treasure each moment and to hold close the people I love. You reminded me of the fragility of life, of the importance of connection, and of living with presence and awareness. These lessons, though they came from loss, will guide me forever.

Ethan, I could not protect or guide you in the way I had hoped. That will always weigh on my heart. But I promise to carry you with me always, to learn from you even now. You were my greatest teacher, and though you are no longer here, your wisdom endures within me. Every step I take forward is in your honor, and every small victory is shared with you. You taught me resilience, the value of family, and the enduring power of love.

I remember how you would begin every family meal with a question, your favorite opening line:

"Hey Grandma, did you know...?" "Hey Granddad, did you know...?" "Hey Mom, did you know...?" "Hey Dad, did you know...?"

Well, Ethan, did you know... I finally wrote the book.

This book is for you, my greatest inspiration, my reason to keep moving forward. It is a collection of lessons on leadership, resilience, and compassion—qualities you embodied so effortlessly. Through these pages, I hope to share the light you brought into my life with others, to carry forward the spirit of love, curiosity, and wisdom you left behind.

You live on in my heart and in all I do, in every lesson I seek to share. I miss you with every breath, and I will love you forever.

TABLE OF CONTENTS

Introduction 9

Part I: Foundational Principles

1. Living in Harmony with Nature 15
2. Finding Balance 23
3. The Strength of Community 31
4. The Role of Personal Relationships 38
5. Rituals of Togetherness 45

Part II: Core Leadership Qualities

6. Respecting Boundaries 53
7. Communication is Key 60
8. Teaching Through Example 68
9. Embracing Diversity 76
10. Developing Future Leaders 82

Part III: The Inner Strength of a Leader

11. Leading with Compassion 90
12. Protecting Your Home 97

13. The Power of Play 104

14. Facing Challenges Together 111

15. Strength in Stillness 118

Part IV: Practices for a Balanced Life

16. The Value of Silence 125

17. Instincts and Intuition 133

18. Simple Pleasures 140

19. Eating Together 147

20. Taking Time to Rest 154

Conclusion 161

About the Author 167

INTRODUCTION

In a world that often celebrates the loudest voices, the quickest results, and the most intense displays of power, there exists a quieter, deeper strength—one that does not seek attention but commands respect through presence and wisdom. This book invites you to explore a different kind of leadership, a form rooted not in conquest or control but in understanding, resilience, and unity. Live and Lead Like a Gorilla takes you on a journey into the wisdom of gorilla life and applies it to the complex art of leadership and personal mastery.

This is not a book of strategies, tactics, or bullet-point advice on achieving power. Instead, it is an invitation to examine leadership through the lens of one of the animal kingdom's most remarkable communities: the gorilla troop. Gorillas, particularly the silverback, embody a leadership style that resonates with a kind of primal wisdom, a deep understanding of balance, connection, and presence. From this natural example, we can draw profound lessons on what it means to lead ourselves and others with strength, compassion, and insight.

Why Gorillas?

Gorillas are not the loudest animals in the jungle, nor the most aggressive. Yet, they are powerful and command a presence that few dare to challenge. They live in cohesive, social groups led by a silverback who embodies a quiet authority. This authority is not enforced through dominance but earned through respect, protection, and care for the troop. The silverback's role is not merely to command but to unite, to create an environment where each member feels secure, valued, and part of a greater whole.

Gorilla leadership is not about constant movement or control; it's about balance. The silverback knows when to stand firm and when to let go, when to act and when to rest, when to defend and when to lead by example. Each chapter in this book draws on these qualities, exploring how we too can cultivate a leadership style that is resilient, compassionate, and deeply aligned with our own values.

True strength doesn't come from overpowering others but from mastering oneself, from living with purpose, integrity, and a fierce independence. The silverback gorilla, in its quiet authority and deep self-knowledge, represents this ideal. It leads not to elevate itself but to uplift the troop, not through coercion but through respect.

This book will challenge the reader to view leadership not as a role, but as a way of being. Each chapter will push you to question conventional notions of strength, to let go of the need for constant validation, and to find power in self-mastery and authentic connection with others. You will learn that leadership is not about shaping others to fit your vision but about creating an environment where each individual's strengths can emerge and thrive.

INTRODUCTION

What You Will Discover

Live and Lead Like a Gorilla is divided into twenty chapters, each one focusing on a unique aspect of gorilla life that offers insights into authentic leadership. You'll learn to embrace strength in stillness, the power of simplicity, and the resilience that comes from facing challenges together. From the importance of rituals, like eating together and taking time to rest, to the power of embracing diversity and cultivating instincts and intuition, each chapter builds on the idea that true leadership is as much about personal integrity as it is about guiding others.

Some of the themes you will encounter include:

- *Living in Harmony with Nature*: Discover how living in balance with our surroundings creates a foundation for authentic leadership. Like gorillas, we thrive when we recognize our interconnectedness and align our actions with respect for the world around us.
- *Embracing Diversity and Individuality*: Learn why strength in leadership lies not in uniformity but in honoring each individual's unique qualities. Gorillas do not seek to mold each other into sameness; instead, they create unity through respect for each individual's role.
- *Teaching by Example:* True leadership is not about telling others what to do but about living your values so fully that others are inspired to follow. You will learn how to embody the qualities you want to see in others.

- *Strength in Stillness and the Power of Silence*: In a society driven by noise, these chapters remind us of the power of quiet reflection, the ability to find calm within chaos, and the silent strength that comes from self-mastery.
- *Taking Time to Rest*: This book's final chapter explores the essential role of rest in maintaining resilience, creativity, and longevity. Leaders who know when to pause, who respect their limits, create a foundation of endurance and perspective that sustains them and their communities.

Each chapter combines practical wisdom with profound insight, inviting you to slow down, to think deeply, and to cultivate a leadership style that is as steady as it is effective.

A Journey of Self-Leadership

At its core, this book is a journey in self-leadership. Just as the silverback's authority rests on self-awareness, restraint, and compassion, the journey of Live and Lead Like a Gorilla is one of inner exploration. It challenges you to cultivate the qualities of patience, wisdom, and presence, qualities that form the bedrock of true resilience. You will learn to lead not only others but yourself, to create a foundation of strength that is grounded, adaptable, and true to who you are.

This journey is not about becoming a different person but about uncovering the leader within—the leader who can balance action with rest, purpose with presence, strength with compassion. Each chapter will guide you deeper into this understanding, using the

INTRODUCTION

metaphor of gorilla life to reveal insights that are universal, timeless, and immediately relevant.

A Call to Authentic Leadership

In an era that often prioritizes speed over depth, control over connection, Live and Lead Like a Gorilla calls us back to the essentials of authentic leadership. It asks us to consider what kind of leaders we want to be—not only in our workplaces but in our communities, our families, and our lives. It encourages us to lead not from ego but from empathy, not from constant motion but from presence, not from the need to be followed but from the desire to create environments where others feel empowered to thrive.

To live and lead like a gorilla is to embrace a life of balance, simplicity, and strength. It is to walk with a quiet confidence that comes from knowing who you are, from valuing connection over control, and from finding fulfillment not only in great achievements but in the simple, powerful moments that make life meaningful.

As you turn the pages of this book, you will be invited to look within yourself, to question what it means to lead and to live in a way that honors both yourself and those around you. May this journey inspire you to lead with wisdom, to live with authenticity, and to find a strength that endures.

Welcome to Live and Lead Like a Gorilla.

PART I: FOUNDATIONAL PRINCIPLES

CHAPTER 1:

LIVING IN HARMONY WITH NATURE

❝❞

Look deep into nature, and then you will understand everything better —Albert Einstein

LIVE AND LEAD LIKE A GORILLA

In the rush of modern life, it's easy to forget that we are part of something much larger than ourselves. Our lives unfold alongside forces far greater than us: the seasons, the cycles of growth and decay, the ebb and flow of natural rhythms that have governed life on this planet for millennia. Yet so often, we find ourselves disconnected from this wisdom, caught up in the human-made world of relentless speed, constant productivity, and a drive to control our surroundings. In leadership and in life, learning to live in harmony with nature offers a way back—a way to reconnect with a deeper purpose, a steadier presence, and a way of leading that is both grounded and sustainable.

Nature, in its vastness, is both a source of inspiration and a profound teacher. For gorillas, life in the wild depends on attunement to these natural cycles. Each member of the troop, from the youngest to the silverback himself, understands their place within a larger whole. They know when to act and when to rest, when to move and when to stay, when to be watchful and when to simply be present. They live in balance, guided by the rhythms of nature, aware that their survival relies on a delicate harmony with their environment.

In leadership, this same sense of harmony can serve as a powerful guide. Living in harmony with nature is not about striving for perfection or controlling every variable. Rather, it's about understanding our place within a larger ecosystem—of people, communities, and relationships—and honoring that interdependence. Leaders who live in harmony with nature understand that their role is not just to direct or drive others but to cultivate an environment where each individual can thrive. They recognize that leadership is not just about guiding others but about fostering balance, resilience, and a sense of shared purpose.

Nature provides countless lessons in resilience, adaptability, and presence. Each ecosystem is a model of balance, a delicate interplay of forces that maintain harmony without force or rigidity. In this way, nature serves as a mirror, reflecting the qualities that are essential for effective leadership. Leaders who seek harmony understand that true strength is found not in controlling others but in creating a space where each person feels seen, valued, and supported.

In the gorilla troop the silverback does not constantly assert his dominance. His presence alone reassures the group, providing a sense of stability and calm. He knows that his role is not to command every movement but to create an environment where his troop feels safe, united, and aligned. This kind of leadership is not about imposing control but about fostering a sense of security and purpose.

As leaders, we can learn from this natural balance. Rather than trying to micromanage or control every aspect of our teams, we can cultivate an atmosphere of trust and mutual respect. Living in harmony with nature means recognizing that each person brings unique strengths and perspectives, and that our role is to guide rather than dictate. By creating a culture of trust, we empower others to contribute fully, fostering a sense of unity that goes beyond individual agendas.

Reflecting on our own leadership, we might ask: Are we creating a space where people feel valued, where they can express their ideas and grow or are we caught in a cycle of over-direction, constantly trying to manage outcomes rather than fostering resilience? Leaders who live in harmony with nature recognize that their influence is not measured by control but by the trust and strength they inspire in others.

Nature is a master of adaptation. Each season brings its own challenges, yet plants and animals adjust, thriving in conditions that are far from static. In leadership, this adaptability is equally vital. Life brings unexpected shifts—moments of growth and seasons of difficulty—and our ability to navigate these changes with grace is a hallmark of resilient leadership.

In the gorilla troop, members do not resist the natural cycles; they adjust to them. When food is plentiful, they gather and thrive together; in times of scarcity, they adapt, moving as needed, conserving energy, and staying close to one another. The silverback leads not by resisting these changes but by responding to them, showing his troop how to weather each season with calm and resilience.

In our own leadership, there is a lesson here: to cultivate the flexibility to adapt to change without losing our sense of purpose. Rather than striving for control, we can focus on developing resilience, building teams that are equipped to handle both the highs and lows with confidence. Living in harmony with nature means acknowledging that change is inevitable, and that true strength is found in adaptability. Leaders who embrace this perspective help their teams remain grounded in times of uncertainty, providing a sense of stability that allows others to feel supported, even amid challenges.

When change comes, we can ask ourselves: Are we holding too tightly to a fixed idea of success, or are we willing to adjust and evolve? Living in harmony with nature invites us to remain open to new paths, to trust that change can bring growth, and to support those we lead in navigating these shifts with confidence and calm.

One of nature's most powerful qualities is its ability to be fully present. The forest does not rush; rivers do not strive to flow faster, and trees do not grow overnight. Each element unfolds at its own pace, guided by a rhythm that is both unhurried and purposeful. In leadership, presence is equally essential. Leaders who are present create an atmosphere of calm and focus, allowing their teams to feel grounded and supported.

In the gorilla troop, the silverback often leads by example through his presence alone. He does not need to constantly intervene or make his presence known; he is simply there, a steady, calming force. This kind of leadership—quiet, observant, and deeply engaged—is a reminder that sometimes the most powerful influence we can have is through our presence, not our words or actions.

As leaders, embracing presence means resisting the impulse to rush or overreact. Instead, we can focus on being fully engaged with each moment, creating a space where people feel seen and heard. Living in harmony with nature is about honoring the value of stillness, the wisdom that comes from allowing ourselves to simply be. Leaders who practice presence bring a sense of calm and clarity to their teams, reminding others that strength does not always require action.

Reflecting on our own presence, we might ask: Are we truly present for those we lead, or are we constantly distracted by the next task, the next goal? Living in harmony with nature encourages us to slow down, to listen more than we speak, and to lead not from urgency but from a place of calm and intentionality.

Nature thrives through interdependence. Each element of an ecosystem plays a role, contributing to the balance and health of the whole. In the same way, effective leadership recognizes the importance of mutual respect, understanding that each person contributes to the team's success. Leaders who honor interdependence create a culture where everyone feels valued, where strengths are celebrated, and where challenges are met together.

In the gorilla troop, this interdependence is evident. The silverback provides protection, but he also relies on the troop members to alert him to danger, to care for the young, to support one another. Each gorilla has a role, and their survival depends on this unity. This shared responsibility, this mutual reliance, strengthens the troop, creating a bond that sustains them even in difficult times.

In our own leadership, recognizing interdependence means valuing each team member's unique contributions, fostering a culture of respect and collaboration. Living in harmony with nature reminds us that success is not achieved alone but through a shared commitment to the collective good. Leaders who embrace interdependence build teams that are resilient, supportive, and united by a common purpose.

As we lead, we might ask ourselves: Do we foster a sense of shared purpose, where everyone feels valued and engaged, or are we focused solely on individual achievement? Living in harmony with nature encourages us to see leadership as a collective effort, a shared journey toward growth and resilience.

At its core, living in harmony with nature is about sustainability—a commitment to a path that respects both our strengths and our limits. Nature does not exhaust itself; it thrives in balance, in a cycle of growth, rest, and renewal. As leaders, adopting a sustainable approach means respecting our own well-being, as well as that of those we lead. It is a reminder that true success is not about relentless pursuit but about creating an environment where each person can thrive.

In the gorilla troop, the silverback knows when to rest, when to conserve energy, when to move forward. He leads by example, showing his troop that strength is not found in constant exertion but in knowing when to pause, to reflect, to renew. This balance—this respect for natural limits—is a lesson in sustainable leadership.

For us, this means creating a culture where balance is valued, where well-being is prioritized, where people feel encouraged to find a rhythm that sustains them. Living in harmony with nature reminds us that leadership is not a sprint but a journey, one that requires resilience, patience, and care.

As we reflect on our path, we might ask ourselves: Are we leading in a way that is sustainable, that respects our own limits and those of our team, or are we pushing beyond what is reasonable? Living in harmony with nature invites us to create a foundation of resilience, a leadership style that is strong, steady, and enduring.

Living in harmony with nature is more than a principle; it is a way of being, a guide that leads us back to ourselves, to a place of balance, connection, and calm. When we embrace this path, we lead not only with strength but with purpose, creating a legacy of leadership that is rooted, resilient, and true.

CHAPTER 2:

FINDING BALANCE

""

Be moderate in order to taste the joys of life in abundance." —Epicurus

The modern leader's world is one of ceaseless striving, where the value of progress has become synonymous with the intensity of the pursuit. We are conditioned to reach further, move faster, and measure success by the speed of our advancement. Yet, in this feverish chase, something vital slips through our fingers—an awareness of what sustains us. Progress without pause becomes exhaustion. Achievement devoid of reflection becomes hollow. To truly lead, we must rethink what it means to find balance, to move forward with a sense of depth, rather than with mere velocity.

Imagine the gorilla in its natural habitat, its presence calm, its movements deliberate. The gorilla does not race against time, nor does it measure its worth in achievements. It lives by an internal rhythm, a cycle that respects both the surge of action and the necessity of rest. In the life of the gorilla, balance is not an ideal; it is a law that governs its existence. It forages only when necessary, moves with purpose, and rests in intervals, conserving energy not out of laziness but as a calculated act of strength. This natural rhythm sustains its vitality and maintains the equilibrium of its surroundings. The gorilla's world reminds us that balance is not found in constant activity but in the wisdom of knowing when to act and when to be still.

As leaders, we often fail to grasp this rhythm. Our ambitions drive us to push forward without respite, to cast aside moments of quiet in favor of action. We become captives of our own desires, mistaking relentless effort for resilience and speed for progress. But nature shows us a different truth: it is in the deliberate pacing of our energy, in the purposeful pauses, that real power lies. The gorilla does not exhaust itself with unnecessary movements; it moves only when movement serves a purpose, rests when rest is required. In this, it exemplifies an unspoken truth that our world, with its obsession for ceaseless output, has forgotten.

Balance, then, is not merely the opposite of activity. It is the foundation that makes action sustainable. In the natural order, imbalance is often catastrophic—a disturbance that weakens the system. The gorilla knows, without needing to be taught, that pushing beyond one's natural limits brings collapse. As leaders, we must learn this lesson, embracing balance not as a weakness but as a strength, an intentional act of preservation that safeguards our capacity to lead. Just as the gorilla lives by an instinctive balance, so must we learn to cultivate a rhythm that serves not only our ambition but also our endurance.

Yet in the modern world, balance feels elusive, a luxury that conflicts with the demands placed upon us. In corporate life, leaders face the expectation to be ever-present, ever-productive, as if value were tied only to activity. This mindset of endless accessibility, of perpetual response to the latest demand, is a recipe for depletion. But pause to consider, balance is not a pause from progress; it is the foundation of progress. It is the bedrock upon which sustainable achievement rests. The gorilla does not act out of urgency; it acts out of purpose. To find balance is to cultivate a similar presence of mind, to approach each action with intent rather than haste.

In the wild, the gorilla does not view rest as an indulgence but as part of life's natural order. There is no guilt in the moments of stillness, no pressure to produce constantly. The gorilla's life reflects a truth our culture often denies, that rest is not idleness, but an essential part of resilience. For leaders, finding balance requires us to discard the belief that value lies only in visible productivity. Productivity, in its truest form, is not endless motion but the ability to choose actions that matter, to focus on the essential rather than the extraneous. When we embrace balance, we no longer seek mere busyness but effective, purposeful work.

This search for balance, however, demands more than simply carving out moments of rest. It requires a rethinking of priorities, a willingness to redefine progress as a journey rather than a sprint. Progress that sacrifices well-being is not true progress; it is merely consumption, a depletion of our own resources. Like the gorilla, who instinctively takes only what it needs, we must learn to be intentional in our efforts. To lead effectively is to understand that balance is not an end but a continuous practice—a discipline of holding on and letting go, of pushing forward and stepping back.

Finding balance also calls for the courage to set boundaries, both for ourselves and for those we lead. The gorilla understands the limits of its own energy, instinctively creating a rhythm that includes moments of intense focus and quiet recovery. It does not need to be reminded to pause, nor does it sacrifice itself for appearances. Leaders, however, are often bound by an invisible chain, feeling compelled to be constantly accessible, ready to respond at any hour. But true leadership requires that we preserve our capacity for meaningful action. Boundaries are not restrictions but protections, shields that allow us to concentrate our strength rather than disperse it needlessly.

In a gorilla troop, these boundaries are instinctual. The members of the troop understand when to move and when to rest, guided by an innate wisdom that ensures their collective survival. They conserve energy not out of weakness but from a profound understanding of balance, a respect for the rhythm that sustains them. As leaders, we too can establish such boundaries—not as barriers, but as structures that uphold our focus and stamina. This might mean protecting time for reflection, setting aside moments free from interruption, or creating a culture where pauses are valued as much as productivity. A leader who respects these rhythms teaches the team to value balance not as an escape from work but as a way to enrich it.

Incorporating balance into leadership also means redefining what success looks like. A balanced team is not one that avoids challenges, nor one that coasts comfortably through tasks. It is a team that understands the power of pacing, that values sustainable effort over fleeting intensity. Like a gorilla troop, whose members rely on one another to maintain stability, a balanced team is cohesive, resilient, and adaptable. Leaders who prioritize this kind of balance cultivate an environment where people can operate at their peak, bringing energy and creativity to their work without burning out. When the leader models balance, the team learns to approach its goals not as a race but as a journey—one that can only be sustained by mutual respect and shared resilience.

Leaders who champion balance understand that productivity and rest are not enemies. They recognize that the ability to pause, to reflect, and to renew one's strength is not a sign of complacency but a testament to wisdom. The gorilla embodies this wisdom, alternating between activity and repose, maintaining a vitality that is undiminished by haste. This rhythm of exertion and recovery is a powerful model for leaders, who too often confuse relentless action with effective leadership. A leader who respects the cycles of energy and renewal fosters an environment where strength is preserved, where clarity replaces fatigue, and where decisions are made from a place of calm rather than urgency.

Balance also requires adaptability—a willingness to respond to the shifting demands of life without losing one's sense of purpose. The gorilla, highly attuned to its environment, adjusts its pace according to need, foraging when resources are plentiful, conserving energy when scarcity requires it. This flexibility allows it to thrive across seasons and circumstances. Leaders, too, must cultivate adaptability, understanding that balance is not a static state but a fluid practice, one that evolves with time and circumstance. Flexibility in leadership is not about abandoning structure but about adjusting one's rhythm in response to the moment. It is a strength that allows leaders to navigate challenges without losing sight of the greater vision.

FINDING BALANCE

In embracing balance, leaders build a foundation that fosters resilience and clarity, qualities essential to long-term success. A leader who prioritizes balance can lead from a place of fullness, with mental clarity, emotional stability, and physical endurance. Teams led in this way experience a shared sense of purpose, a connection that goes beyond mere productivity. When people feel that their well-being is valued, they are more likely to engage fully, to innovate freely, and to remain loyal to shared goals. Balance, then, is not a retreat from leadership but a deepening of it—a path that builds trust and fuels creativity, creating an environment where people feel empowered to give their best.

At its core, finding balance in leadership is about aligning action with intention, shaping progress around a foundation of inner strength. It is the willingness to lead not by force but by example, to demonstrate that success need not come at the expense of self. The gorilla's life embodies this principle, its movements guided not by external pressures but by a profound inner equilibrium. In seeking balance, we too honor our own limits, valuing both our drive and our need for renewal. Leadership is not about endlessly pushing forward but about moving forward with awareness, building strength through reflection as much as through action.

To live and lead with balance is to recognize that sustainable success lies in harmony, not in dominance. It is a quiet strength, a form of power that does not demand constant proof. Leaders who find this balance are free from the illusions of urgency, free to act from a place of clarity rather than compulsion. They understand that leadership is not about leading others in an endless chase, but about creating a rhythm that others can follow, a tempo that honors both progress and pause. True balance in leadership is not a retreat but a mastery of presence, a testament to the wisdom of knowing when to move and when to remain still.

In the end, finding balance is about embracing our role as leaders with humility and strength. Just as the gorilla moves through its world with a steady awareness, so must we cultivate an inner balance that guides us through the demands of leadership. This path is not one of compromise, but of conviction—a commitment to lead in a way that nourishes both our ambition and our well-being. To live and lead like a gorilla is to understand that the highest form of strength lies not in constant motion but in the power to choose when to act, when to rest, and when to simply be.

CHAPTER 3:

THE STRENGTH OF COMMUNITY

❝❞

"The greatness of a community is most accurately measured by the compassionate actions of its members." —Coretta Scott King

We speak of community as a source of strength, but often, we remain distant from its true meaning. We celebrate individual accomplishments, applaud personal success, and cherish solitary achievements as if they alone bear value. Yet real leadership—effective, grounded, and visionary—requires more than the feats of a single individual. It arises from the energy of the community, a force that magnifies each member's potential, elevating the whole above the sum of its parts. Community is not merely a backdrop for individual greatness; it is the foundation upon which enduring success is built.

Picture the gorilla troop in the wild. Here, every member serves a role, each contributing to the welfare of the group with an unspoken understanding that their survival and strength rely on one another. The silverback may lead, but he is not independent of the troop. His strength, his authority, and his power emerge not solely from his own prowess but from the presence and unity of his community. In their togetherness, they forge a strength that transcends the capabilities of any single gorilla. The mothers nurture, the youth learn and explore, and even the elder gorillas bring wisdom and stability. There is no competition for dominance here; rather, there is an understanding that power flows from unity, from mutual respect, and from the unwavering commitment each has to the collective whole.

The silverback's leadership is not about personal achievement. His influence does not come from constant displays of power or dominance. His true strength lies in the trust he places in his troop, in his ability to lead by fostering a secure, interconnected community. Each member relies on the others, each role matters, and each action taken is not for individual gain but for the collective good. Leaders, too, can learn from this. Leadership does not rest on individual accomplishments but on the ability to create an environment where every person's strength contributes to a larger purpose.

To lead is not to possess all the answers or to be the mightiest figure. It is to build a foundation of trust, empowering those around you to act with purpose and autonomy. In the modern world, the concept of leadership often defaults to authority—a projection of singular power and control. Yet this is a hollow path, one that breeds isolation rather than strength. The gorilla troop teaches us that strength is not found in lone pursuits but in the bonds we form and nurture. The silverback leads not by overshadowing others but by creating an environment where everyone can thrive, where each member's contributions are respected, and where the collective strength exceeds that of any one individual.

Imagine the communities you belong to—whether they are teams at work, families, or social circles. Are these communities united by trust and shared purpose, or are they mere collections of individuals, each striving alone? To build a strong community is to understand that success is not a solitary path. True leadership looks beyond the self, recognizing that each person's role matters, that individual victories are amplified when they contribute to the collective strength of the group. Leaders must be vigilant against the temptation to focus solely on their own progress. They must instead look to the bonds they form, the trust they build, and the unity they foster.

Consider the silverback's understanding: his strength is amplified, not diminished, by the support of the troop. He does not lead through relentless control but through a careful balance of guidance and trust. He knows his power is not threatened by the growth of others; rather, it is solidified by it. As leaders, we should reflect on our own approach. Do we create an environment where each individual's strengths are celebrated and valued, or do we treat people as replaceable parts, interchangeable and disposable? The strength of any community lies in its bonds, its shared support, and the respect that connects its members.

Reflecting on our roles within communities brings us to a critical question: Do we contribute to the well-being of the group, or do we view it as a platform for our own achievements? To embrace community is to rise above the self, to recognize that success—lasting, meaningful success—is born from collaboration and mutual respect. The gorilla troop moves as one, each individual acting not out of obligation but out of an instinctive understanding that their personal well-being is inseparably tied to the group. This interdependence, this unity, is a lesson we are often quick to forget in our pursuit of personal success.

THE STRENGTH OF COMMUNITY

When leading a team, ask yourself if you trust those around you, if you create a space where they can act with purpose, or if you undermine this by assuming their roles as your own. A community's strength is a reflection of the bonds its members share. In times of ease, these bonds may seem trivial, yet in moments of adversity, they become the foundation upon which resilience is built. The silverback, aware of his role, does not attempt to outshine the others but protects and empowers them, creating a stable environment where each member can find purpose and security.

Strengthening a community is not the work of a moment. It is a continuous process, built through deliberate choices and sustained by mutual respect. In the gorilla troop, bonds form and solidify through daily rituals—moments of grooming, shared play, and protective gestures. Leaders, too, must build these connections intentionally, fostering an environment where trust is given as freely as it is earned. These bonds are not built-in grand gestures but in the simple, consistent acts of appreciation, the small moments of connection that lay the foundation for something lasting and meaningful.

But a community's true strength is tested in times of hardship. In good times, unity is effortless; in times of struggle, it is essential. In the face of danger, the silverback does not stand alone; he is supported by the strength of the troop. A leader, too, must recognize that challenges are not a call to isolate oneself, to assume every burden, but an opportunity to draw upon the collective strength of the group. It is in these moments that the power of community becomes undeniable. Leadership is not about facing challenges alone but about enabling the group to stand together, each member contributing to the resolution, each role significant in the effort to overcome.

A resilient community is not merely one that endures; it is one that emerges stronger from adversity. When we build trust, when we foster a culture of support, challenges no longer feel insurmountable. We find security in the knowledge that we are not alone, that we are surrounded by those who share in our vision and are committed to seeing it through. Within the gorilla troop, each generation learns from the last. The young observe the old, absorbing wisdom through quiet observation. This unspoken mentorship ensures the troop's survival and growth, passing resilience from one generation to the next.

Leadership, too, must be mindful of legacy. Every action, every decision, every moment of unity serves as an example, an unspoken lesson that resonates beyond the present. The example we set is not one of mere authority, but of connection, of mutual respect, of shared responsibility. True leadership values the strength of community, recognizing that our actions, our words, and our attitudes will shape those who follow. The impact of a leader is seen not in the heights they reach alone but in the depth and cohesion of the community they leave behind.

THE STRENGTH OF COMMUNITY

In our leadership journeys, let us consider: Are we creating environments where others feel valued, where the collective success is prioritized above personal glory? Are we lifting others up, strengthening the bonds that hold the community together? True leadership is reflected not in isolated achievements but in the shared progress of a group that feels connected, appreciated, and inspired. The gorilla's strength lies not in isolation but in the community that surrounds it, the connections that bind it, and the shared purpose that drives it forward.

To lead like a gorilla is to understand that leadership is not a solitary pursuit. It is a communal path, one that requires us to honor each member's role, to build trust, and to foster a culture of respect and interdependence. This kind of leadership creates communities that are resilient, adaptable, and deeply interconnected. When we lead with the strength of community, we create something that endures—something that holds power, meaning, and purpose beyond the achievements of any one individual.

The legacy of leadership is not defined by personal accomplishments but by the collective impact we inspire. To embrace this mindset is to recognize that true strength lies not in standing apart but in standing within, to understand that our individual purpose finds its highest expression when it serves the greater whole.

CHAPTER 4:

THE ROLE OF PERSONAL RELATIONSHIPS

❝❞

"People will forget what you said, people will forget what you did, but people will never forget how you made them feel." —Maya Angelou

THE ROLE OF PERSONAL RELATIONSHIPS

Leadership is often viewed through the lens of achievement—results, influence, accomplishments. Yet these are only the outward markers of leadership. The real essence, the quiet power that underpins all effective leadership, is found in the relationships we cultivate. It is in the unseen bonds, the unspoken loyalties, and the steadfast presence that leadership truly reveals itself. Just as a tree's strength lies in its roots rather than its height, so too does the leader's strength lie in the depth of their personal relationships.

In the life of a gorilla troop, these personal bonds are not just beneficial; they are essential. The silverback does not command his troop through raw force alone but through an emotional connection that reassures and protects each member. His strength is matched by his empathy, a compassion that unites the troop and binds them to him. This connection fosters an environment of security, where each gorilla finds its place, knowing it belongs and is valued. The silverback's presence alone communicates trust, a reassurance that each member is safe and supported, even in times of uncertainty.

Leadership is not a position to wield but a relationship to nurture. To truly lead is to understand that people are not simply roles to fill or resources to manage—they are individuals with lives, aspirations, fears, and strengths. Leadership that values personal relationships creates a culture where people feel seen and valued. They are not merely instruments of productivity but partners in a shared journey. This perspective does more than achieve goals; it inspires loyalty, resilience, and unity.

Think of the people in your life. Are your connections with them based on what they can offer you, or do they rest on a deeper foundation of trust and respect? When we build relationships based solely on utility, we reduce individuals to roles, diminishing both their potential and ours. But relationships that are nurtured with intention and care become sources of strength. The silverback does not regard his troop as mere followers; they are his family. He leads them with an understanding that goes beyond words, a trust that they are all part of something larger than themselves.

For the gorilla, relationships serve as a protective force, a bond that transforms individuals into a united group capable of facing any challenge. The presence of the silverback assures the troop of its security, a security that is not based on words or commands but on presence and constancy. In leadership, this sense of security is invaluable. A leader who builds relationships based on trust and empathy creates an environment where people feel safe to be themselves, to take risks, and to grow. This safety is not an absence of challenge; it is the foundation that allows people to confront challenges without fear of abandonment or betrayal.

When we consider the relationships in our own lives, we must ask ourselves if they serve as sources of strength or if they are weighed down by doubt and uncertainty. Do we create spaces where others feel safe to contribute their true selves, or are they left unsure of their place in our world? True leadership is not about asserting power but about empowering others. It is about creating relationships that lift

THE ROLE OF PERSONAL RELATIONSHIPS

people, not because they serve our immediate needs but because they hold intrinsic value. Relationships are the conduit through which influence flows, the unseen bonds that connect people to a common vision and give purpose to shared work.

The silverback's role in the troop is not just to protect; it is to nurture. He does not see his members as tools to be wielded but as integral parts of the whole. His leadership is a blend of strength and compassion, a dual force that reassures each member of their place and purpose. As leaders, we can learn from this approach. Personal relationships are not created by authority; they are built through empathy, trust, and a commitment to the well-being of others. This depth of connection transforms leadership from mere direction into inspiration.

In our modern world, where the value of relationships is often reduced to networking, we risk forgetting the power of true connection. Relationships are not just exchanges; they are partnerships in which each person's strengths, challenges, and potential are recognized and valued. They are not built through single encounters but through consistent, genuine interactions that reinforce trust over time. Just as the gorilla troop builds bonds through daily acts of grooming, play, and shared watchfulness, so too must we build connections through gestures of care, respect, and appreciation.

Consider the relationships you hold dear. What defines them? Is it the benefits they bring, or the mutual respect and understanding that lies within them? Leadership is not about gathering followers or leveraging connections; it is about building bonds that endure, bonds that can be relied upon in both triumph and adversity. The silverback leads with the understanding that his strength is not in solitude but in the presence of others. He does not seek dominance over his troop; he seeks unity with them. He is their protector, their guide, and in return, he has their loyalty and trust.

True relationships in leadership also provide a foundation for conflict resolution. In any group, misunderstandings will arise, and how a leader handles these moments often defines the strength of the team. A leader who values relationships approaches conflict with empathy and patience. They listen not to argue but to understand. They recognize that most conflicts are not about the surface issue but about deeper needs and emotions. By addressing these underlying concerns, they resolve conflicts in a way that strengthens, rather than divides, the team.

Imagine a leader who, instead of reacting defensively, invites both parties in a disagreement to share their perspectives fully. This approach, grounded in empathy, opens the door to meaningful resolution. Each person feels heard, respected, and the outcome becomes one that honors each individual's dignity. This is the power of compassionate leadership—it does not avoid difficult conversations; it approaches them with care, seeking to honor relationships above personal pride.

THE ROLE OF PERSONAL RELATIONSHIPS

The role of relationships is also crucial when supporting those who are struggling. In any group, there will be times when individuals face personal challenges that affect their performance. A leader who values relationships responds with understanding and support. They offer flexibility when needed, check in regularly, and provide resources that help. This approach does not compromise accountability; rather, it honors the humanity of each person. When people feel that they are valued beyond their contributions, they find resilience within themselves, and their loyalty to the leader and the team deepens.

For the silverback, this role is instinctual. He does not judge or ignore a struggling member but provides the reassurance of his presence. This act of compassion builds a foundation of trust within the troop, a trust that assures each gorilla that they are part of something greater. Leaders who adopt this approach create environments where people feel secure enough to reach out, to ask for help, and to offer support to others. In such communities, people thrive because they know that they are valued as whole individuals.

Trust is the foundation of any strong relationship, and compassionate leadership cultivates this trust by showing people that they matter. It is easy to trust a leader who demonstrates genuine care, who takes the time to understand individual needs, and who prioritizes the well-being of the team over personal accolades. This trust is not built overnight; it is nurtured through consistent acts of kindness and support. Over time, it becomes the bedrock upon which the team stands, uniting them in purpose and resilience.

The role of personal relationships in leadership extends beyond immediate interactions to shape the broader culture of an organization. Compassionate leaders inspire others to lead with empathy, creating a ripple effect that influences how people treat one another. When leaders prioritize relationships, they set a standard for kindness, respect, and support, fostering a culture where these values become the norm. This creates a legacy of care and connection that echoes beyond any one individual.

To lead through personal relationships is to recognize that each person we encounter has a unique story, a world of experiences that shapes who they are. Leadership is not about commanding authority but about creating connection. Just as the silverback leads his troop with strength and compassion, we too can create teams that thrive on trust, empathy, and respect. By embracing personal relationships, we go beyond managing tasks and goals. We build communities where people feel valued, supported, and inspired to do their best work.

When we lead through relationships, we leave a legacy that transcends our own lives. We become leaders who are remembered not only for what we achieved but for the way we made people feel. This is the heart of leadership—not in the power we hold, but in the lives we touch.

CHAPTER 5:

RITUALS OF TOGETHERNESS

❝❞

"The strongest bonds are forged in the fires of shared moments and traditions."
—*Anonymous*

In leadership, we often focus on strategy, goals, and the drive to inspire others. But there exists an equally powerful, often underestimated force at the heart of any cohesive team: the rituals of togetherness. Togetherness does not come by chance; it is carefully cultivated through shared moments, mutual respect, and the simple yet profound power of ritual. These small, consistent acts of connection are the foundation of strong, enduring communities.

Look to a gorilla troop for an example. Every day, the members come together in ways that reinforce their bonds. Whether through grooming, resting close to one another, or engaging in play, they participate in rituals that unify them. These aren't random actions; they are intentional, consistent behaviors that foster security, harmony, and belonging. The silverback doesn't enforce these rituals—they occur naturally, forming a network of trust and stability that ensures the troop's strength. The health of the community is sustained through these regular acts of connection, creating a rhythm that anchors each member's place within the group.

As leaders, we, too, have the opportunity to cultivate rituals of togetherness within our teams, families, or communities. This doesn't mean establishing rigid schedules or formal processes. It means intentionally creating moments of connection that remind people they are seen, valued, and part of something larger. When people feel connected, they are more likely to work together, trust one another, and push forward when challenges arise. These rituals are the glue that binds individuals into a cohesive, resilient community.

RITUALS OF TOGETHERNESS

The impact of these rituals lies in the sense of security they foster. The silverback, even in moments of calm, doesn't need to constantly oversee his troop because the trust and unity are woven into their daily interactions. In the same way, when we build rituals of togetherness, they become anchors—touchstones we return to, especially in uncertain or chaotic times. These shared practices serve as roots, giving us a sense of stability and continuity.

Think about the routines that already exist in your life—a weekly family dinner, a regular team meeting, or a simple daily coffee with a friend or colleague. These moments are not just appointments; they are opportunities for connection. A leader's role is to recognize the value of these rituals, to cultivate an environment where they are given space to flourish. When people feel consistently connected to one another, their engagement deepens, and they become more committed to the team, family, or community they belong to.

It's all too easy to let the demands of daily life overshadow these rituals. But when we neglect these moments, the consequences emerge subtly but surely. In a team, the lack of regular check-ins allows small issues to grow into larger problems. In families, missed dinners or skipped traditions create a feeling of distance, eroding the closeness that bonds members. Just as a gorilla troop becomes vulnerable when its members stop engaging in their daily rituals, so do we lose our sense of unity when we stop making time for each other.

There is beauty in the simplicity of these rituals. A gorilla troop doesn't need grand occasions to come together. Instead, their daily acts—small, repeated, intentional—are the lifeblood of their social fabric. The same is true for us. We don't need elaborate events or celebrations to reinforce our connections. It's in the small, everyday moments that the deepest bonds are forged. These rituals are the quiet, powerful threads that hold us together, even when we don't realize it.

Building rituals of togetherness can start with something simple. It might be a morning team huddle where everyone shares their goals for the day or a weekly check-in where each person has a moment to speak freely. These rituals don't have to be complex; the power lies in their consistency. In family life, rituals can be as simple as a Sunday breakfast, a walk after dinner, or an evening spent reading together. These shared experiences create a rhythm that people can depend on, a sense of belonging and continuity that withstands the ebb and flow of life.

Consistency is the bedrock of strong teams, families, and communities. The silverback doesn't question the value of his daily routines, and neither should we. When we commit to these rituals, we create an environment of loyalty, trust, and stability. Through shared experiences, bonds are strengthened, and a sense of belonging grows. These small but powerful rituals become the foundation of communities that are resilient, adaptable, and deeply connected.

The simplicity of these rituals does not diminish their significance. On the contrary, their unassuming nature is what gives them their strength. Think about the last time you felt truly connected to someone. It likely wasn't during a grand event but in a small, shared moment—perhaps a conversation, a laugh, or a shared silence. These

RITUALS OF TOGETHERNESS

are the moments that matter, and as leaders, it is our role to make space for them. When we focus on these seemingly small interactions, we reinforce the foundation upon which all trust is built.

In a professional setting, these rituals may seem secondary to productivity, but the truth is that productivity flourishes in environments where people feel valued and connected. A team bonded by trust and shared purpose is a team that performs at its best. The same is true in family life. Our loved ones thrive when they feel valued, safe, and understood. These feelings do not appear by accident—they are cultivated through the intentional, consistent rituals of togetherness that we prioritize.

It's important to remember that these rituals are not just beneficial during times of ease. In fact, they are most crucial during difficult moments. A gorilla troop bands together when faced with a threat, relying on the strength of their unity. Similarly, when a team or family encounters obstacles, the rituals they have established become the foundation that holds them steady. In challenging times, people lean on the bonds they trust, and if those bonds have been nurtured, they will find the resilience to face adversity together.

A leader who invests in these rituals will find their team united in moments of crisis. There's no need for grand gestures of reassurance; the trust is already there. People don't question your commitment because they know, through the consistency of your actions, that you care about them. This trust isn't built in a single day; it is the cumulative result of everyday rituals that demonstrate a leader's dedication to the group.

Consider the most successful teams, organizations, or families you know. Likely, they have rituals that bring them together consistently. They do not wait for crises to build unity. Instead, they establish a foundation of connection that is present in every moment, providing stability in both calm and storm. This foundation is something we can all strive to create, whether in our professional lives or personal relationships.

These rituals of togetherness build something far greater than the sum of their parts. The silverback does not engage in these acts solely for himself; he understands that his strength is intertwined with the unity of the group. The same is true for us. Our success, both in leadership and in life, is rooted in the relationships we foster and the community we create around us. We flourish when we prioritize one another, when we make time for connection, and when we understand that these bonds are the essence of resilience.

Reflect on your own role as a leader—whether in your workplace, your family, or your community. What rituals of togetherness are you nurturing? Are you creating opportunities for connection, for shared experiences, for moments that remind people of their worth? If not, what small steps can you take to begin? Leadership is not about how much you can accomplish alone; it is about how well you bring people together. Like the gorillas, we thrive when we are connected, when we recognize the value of each person, and when we nurture the bonds that hold us together.

By focusing on rituals of togetherness, we create communities that are not only more resilient but more meaningful. When challenges arise, as they inevitably will, the relationships we have cultivated become our greatest asset. It is through these moments of connection that true leadership and success are rooted.

In the end, rituals of togetherness do more than create strong teams and families; they create legacies. Leaders who invest in these small acts of connection leave behind communities that are capable of thriving beyond their own presence. The rituals we build today become the traditions that carry forward, binding future generations with the same strength and resilience we cultivated.

As you move forward, consider this: What legacy are you creating through the rituals you build? Are you setting an example of unity, of mutual respect, of shared purpose? To lead effectively is to understand that these rituals, these moments of togetherness, are not just parts of the journey—they are the journey. They are what give leadership its depth, its meaning, and its power.

To lead like a gorilla is to recognize that strength does not lie in isolation but in the bonds we nurture. It is to understand that true leadership is found in the quiet moments of connection, the shared rituals that remind us of our place within something greater. When we invest in these rituals of togetherness, we build a foundation that sustains, inspires, and endures. This is the essence of leadership. This is the power of unity.

PART II: CORE LEADERSHIP QUALITIES

CHAPTER 6:

RESPECTING BOUNDARIES

❝❞

"Good fences make good neighbors."
—*Robert Frost*

Boundaries are often misunderstood as limitations, restrictions that keep us from achieving our full potential. But true boundaries are not walls meant to confine; they are lines that define us, guiding us toward our higher purpose. Boundaries are a declaration of self, a statement of identity that says, "This is who I am, and this is where I stand." In leadership, understanding boundaries—both our own and those of others—is essential to building communities that respect individuality while fostering unity.

The gorilla troop exemplifies this balance. Each member of the troop has an instinctual sense of where they stand, of what they contribute, and of where their roles begin and end. The silverback, powerful yet self-contained, does not impose himself upon others without reason. He moves within a clear boundary, maintaining his authority not by crossing lines unnecessarily but by respecting the space of each member. His influence is not forced; it flows naturally from his understanding of boundaries, from knowing when to act and when to allow others their own space. This respect for boundaries within the troop is not a mark of weakness; it is the foundation of their strength.

In leadership, boundaries are not merely about protecting one's time or energy—they are about self-mastery. A leader who cannot set and respect boundaries is like a river that spills over its banks, flooding everything in its path. Boundaries channel power, directing it with precision, ensuring that each action taken is purposeful rather than haphazard. In a world that celebrates boundless ambition

RESPECTING BOUNDARIES

and constant availability, boundaries become an act of rebellion, a means of preserving one's strength and authenticity. To lead with true strength, we must first learn to honor the lines that define us, for it is within these lines that our power resides.

Consider the boundaries in your own life. Are they clear and respected, or are they constantly crossed in the name of productivity or obligation? Do you allow others to encroach upon your time, your energy, your very essence, believing that self-sacrifice is the mark of a good leader? The truth is that no one can lead effectively if they are constantly drained, if their sense of self is eroded by the demands of others. Boundaries are not selfish; they are acts of respect—both for oneself and for those around us. By defining what we will and will not allow, we create a space where our best self can emerge.

In the gorilla troop, boundaries are understood intuitively. The young know when to approach the silverback and when to keep their distance. The mothers guard their young, carving out spaces of safety without needing permission. Each member respects the space of the others, creating a fluid harmony that allows the troop to function as a unit without sacrificing individuality. This respect is not taught; it is felt. It arises from an understanding that true strength does not come from dominance but from coexistence, from the recognition that each member's space and role are essential to the whole.

As leaders, we must cultivate this same respect. We cannot command respect if we do not first respect ourselves. And to respect ourselves, we must be willing to set boundaries that preserve our integrity. This may mean saying no to demands that drain us or stepping back when our presence is not necessary. It may mean allowing others to take the lead, trusting that their strength will complement ours. Boundaries are not barriers to connection; they are the framework within which connection can flourish. When we set and honor boundaries, we teach others to do the same, creating a culture of mutual respect.

Boundaries also serve as a test of character. In the presence of boundaries, we reveal our true nature: Do we seek to control others, or do we respect their autonomy? Do we impose ourselves, or do we trust in the strength of others? The silverback does not assert his dominance through constant interference; he trusts the natural order of the troop, knowing that his authority is strongest when it is not imposed. True leadership is not about exerting control but about empowering others to find their own strength within the boundaries we mutually respect.

In today's world, boundaries are often viewed as weaknesses, as signs of limitation. But boundaries are not weaknesses; they are the lines that shape our potential. Without boundaries, we become scattered, pulled in every direction, unable to focus our strength. Consider a river without banks; it loses its form, its power, its very essence. Boundaries are the banks that direct the river of our leadership, allowing us to channel our energy with clarity and purpose. When we respect our own boundaries, we protect our strength, preserving it for the moments that matter.

RESPECTING BOUNDARIES

Reflect on the boundaries you set—or fail to set—in your own life. Do you allow others to define your time, your priorities, your sense of self? Or do you stand firm, defining yourself through the choices you make and the lines you draw? Leadership requires a willingness to say, "This is my limit." It is not an act of defiance; it is an act of self-preservation. To lead effectively, we must first lead ourselves, and self-leadership begins with the courage to establish boundaries that honor our true nature.

In the gorilla troop, boundaries are also a means of protection. The silverback defends the troop's space, warding off external threats not out of aggression but out of respect for the integrity of his community. He does not seek conflict, but he does not avoid it when necessary. Boundaries are not walls to hide behind; they are lines of strength that declare, "This is where we stand." As leaders, we must cultivate this protective strength, not only defending our own boundaries but also respecting the boundaries of others. In doing so, we create a culture of mutual respect, a community where each person's space is honored.

Boundaries also serve to strengthen relationships. Paradoxically, it is through boundaries that we find true connection. When we respect the space of others, we show that we value their autonomy, that we do not seek to impose our will upon them. This respect fosters trust, creating an environment where people feel safe to be themselves. The silverback does not micromanage his troop; he allows each member the space to fulfill their role, knowing that their contribution is vital. This trust, this respect for boundaries, is what allows the troop to function as a cohesive unit.

In leadership, respecting boundaries is a form of humility. It is a recognition that we are not all things to all people, that our strength lies not in our ability to do everything but in our ability to do what matters most. Boundaries force us to confront our limitations, to acknowledge that we are not infinite. But in this acknowledgment, we find freedom. We find the space to focus on what truly matters, to lead with intention rather than exhaustion. Boundaries are not prisons; they are pathways to purpose.

To respect boundaries is to embrace our own nature and the nature of others. It is to understand that we each have our own path, our own space, our own purpose. In the gorilla troop, this understanding is instinctual. The silverback does not overstep his role, nor does he allow others to overstep theirs. He leads by example, showing that strength is not found in the erosion of boundaries but in their preservation. To lead like the silverback is to know where we end and others begin, to understand that our power is greatest when it is contained within the lines we choose.

As you reflect on your own journey, consider the boundaries that define you. Are they boundaries you set with intention, or are they lines imposed by the demands of others? Do you respect the boundaries of those around you, or do you seek to mold them to your own vision? Leadership is not about erasing boundaries but about honoring them. It is about understanding that true strength arises not from the conquest of others but from the mastery of oneself.

RESPECTING BOUNDARIES

Boundaries are not limitations; they are definitions. They are the lines that give shape to our potential, the parameters within which we find our true power. To respect boundaries is to respect the essence of leadership itself—a balance between autonomy and unity, between strength and restraint. Like the silverback, we must lead with both power and humility, respecting the lines that allow each person, each role, to flourish.

To lead effectively is to understand that boundaries are not the edges of our potential but the foundation of it. They are not the limits of our power but the channels through which it flows. When we respect boundaries, we respect the nature of strength itself—a strength that does not consume but contains, that does not dominate but empowers.

In this understanding, we find the essence of leadership. We find the courage to stand firm, the wisdom to step back, and the strength to let others step forward. To lead with boundaries is to lead with integrity, to build communities where autonomy is honored, and unity is forged not through force but through mutual respect. This is the power of boundaries. This is the path to true leadership.

CHAPTER 7:

COMMUNICATION IS KEY

"Wise men speak because they have something to say; fools because they have to say something."
—Plato

Leadership often brings to mind power, vision, and decisiveness. But none of these qualities matter if a leader cannot communicate effectively. Communication is the lifeblood of any community, a thread that weaves together individual intentions, shared goals, and collective strength. Without it, even the most skilled team will fracture, unable to act as a cohesive whole. Leadership, then, is not about constant talking, nor is it about forcing others to listen. It is about knowing what to say, how to listen, and when silence speaks louder than words.

Within a gorilla troop, communication is constant but rarely verbal in the human sense. It is rooted in presence, gesture, and a deep understanding that transcends mere words. The silverback, as the leader, does not impose his authority through loud proclamations. His influence is subtle yet profound, communicated through his posture, his gaze, and his movement. When he looks, they see; when he stands, they follow. This form of communication is not about noise or volume; it is about clarity, about conveying meaning with precision and purpose. In the silence of a gorilla troop, there is a wealth of communication, a silent yet powerful language that binds them as one.

As leaders, we can learn from this simplicity. Communication is not about filling the air with words; it is about connecting with others in a way that fosters trust, understanding, and action. Many leaders mistakenly believe that effective communication means asserting their ideas, making their voice the loudest in the room. But true communication—the kind that inspires and unites—requires much more listening than speaking. It demands the willingness to understand before being understood, to create space for others to contribute, and to honor the silence where insight often emerges.

Consider the communication within your own leadership. Do you speak to be heard, or do you listen to understand? Are your words meant to connect or to command? In leadership, communication is not a one-way flow; it is a bridge that connects individuals to a shared vision. When communication is centered on connection rather than control, people feel valued. They become more willing to contribute, more open to collaboration, and more invested in the shared mission.

In a gorilla troop, the silverback's authority is communicated with subtlety and respect. He does not need to assert himself constantly, nor does he require affirmation of his status. His leadership is known and felt, not through grand speeches or displays but through his presence and the quiet assurance he brings. When the troop senses danger, he may offer a low growl, a sound that is both a warning and a reassurance. This simple sound speaks volumes; it tells the troop to stay close, to remain calm, to trust in his protection. The silverback's communication is not constant, yet it is continuous—always there, a presence that guides without overwhelming.

In our own lives, we often forget that communication is more than words. Body language, tone, and timing are as much a part of the message as the words themselves. A leader's silence can convey

COMMUNICATION IS KEY

strength and patience, while an ill-timed comment can erode trust. Communication, then, is an art as much as it is a skill. The leader who masters it does so not by talking more but by listening deeply, by understanding the nuances of interaction, and by creating a space where everyone feels heard.

Reflect on the power of silence in communication. Are you comfortable with pauses, with giving others room to think and respond? Or do you feel the need to fill every silence, believing that leadership requires constant direction? Silence is not emptiness; it is an invitation. In the pause, there is space for thought, for reflection, for others to step forward. Just as the silverback allows his presence to communicate, a wise leader learns to use silence to foster insight, to give others room to share their voices.

In a team, communication is the foundation of trust. Without trust, words become empty, directives feel hollow, and connections weaken. A gorilla troop relies on unspoken bonds, a trust that each member's signals are genuine, that each gesture is sincere. Trust in communication is not built through charisma or clever words; it is built through consistency, through the quiet assurance that what is said reflects what is felt. Leaders who prioritize genuine communication build teams where trust flows naturally, where words carry weight because they are grounded in truth.

Communication is also essential for conflict resolution. In any group, misunderstandings will arise, and how a leader communicates in these moments often determines the outcome. A leader who values communication does not react impulsively but listens to understand the perspectives involved. They do not assume they know the answer; they open themselves to hearing it. The silverback, when faced with tension within the troop, does not respond with aggression. He intervenes with calmness, his posture and gaze communicating the need for unity rather than division. His very presence reminds the troop of their bond, allowing tension to dissolve in the light of mutual respect.

Imagine the impact of approaching conflict with this level of composure and openness. When leaders listen without judgment, they create an environment where differences can be addressed rather than buried. True communication does not shy away from conflict; it embraces it as an opportunity to deepen understanding and strengthen bonds. A leader who communicates with empathy and patience transforms conflict from a barrier into a bridge, a moment of division into a chance for unity.

Consider the role of empathy in communication. Do you speak to assert your position, or do you seek to understand the experiences of others? Communication that lacks empathy becomes hollow, a series of words with no connection. In the gorilla troop, empathy is expressed through touch, through proximity, through the way each member responds to the needs of the others. When a young gorilla is distressed, the silverback may place a gentle hand upon its back—a silent act that speaks of reassurance, of shared feeling. This empathy, this willingness to connect without words, is the foundation of their unity.

As leaders, we must learn to communicate with this same empathy. It is not enough to instruct or direct; we must also understand and acknowledge. Empathy in communication means recognizing that every individual carries their own burdens, that behind every interaction is a world of experiences. When we communicate with empathy, we show that we value not only the task but the person. This fosters loyalty and commitment, creating a team that feels seen, respected, and valued.

True communication also means knowing when to speak with conviction and when to allow others to lead the conversation. The silverback does not dominate every interaction; he knows when to step forward and when to step back. His leadership is balanced by his restraint, his understanding that communication is not about control but about connection. A leader who speaks only to assert their authority erodes the very trust they seek to build. But a leader who speaks with purpose and clarity creates a foundation of respect.

Reflect on your own communication style. Are you willing to listen as intently as you speak? Are you open to feedback, to perspectives that challenge your own? A leader who listens more than they speak, who values input as much as output, creates a team that feels empowered. They foster an environment where people contribute openly, where ideas are shared freely, and where innovation thrives. Communication is not a one-way street; it is a dialogue, a continuous exchange that brings depth and diversity to the team.

In times of crisis, communication becomes even more vital. When uncertainty looms, when tension is high, a leader's words and actions carry greater weight. In these moments, a leader's communication must be both steady and reassuring. The silverback's calm in the face of danger is a message in itself—a message of strength, of assurance, of quiet confidence. His demeanor tells the troop that they are safe, that they are together, that they will face the challenge as one.

In your own leadership, consider how you communicate in times of uncertainty. Do you project calm and confidence, or do you allow your own fears to amplify the anxiety of those around you? Communication in crisis is not about hiding the truth; it is about offering stability. It is about providing a clear direction, a steady presence that others can rely upon. The leader who communicates with calm in crisis creates a foundation of resilience, a space where people can find strength even in the face of the unknown.

Ultimately, communication is about respect. Respect for the team, for the individual, for the vision. When leaders communicate with respect, they foster an environment where everyone feels valued. In the gorilla troop, every member has a voice, even if it is not expressed in words. Each movement, each gesture, is acknowledged. This respect, this attention to each member's presence, is what makes the troop strong. As leaders, when we communicate with respect, we create a culture where people feel seen, where they know their voices matter.

To lead effectively is to communicate with purpose, clarity, and respect. It is to understand that communication is not just about words; it is about presence, empathy, and the willingness to connect.

COMMUNICATION IS KEY

Like the silverback, we must learn to lead with both silence and speech, to let our actions speak as powerfully as our words, and to build communities where communication is a bridge, not a barrier.

As you reflect on your own approach to communication, ask yourself: Are your words building connections or creating distance? Are you listening as much as you speak? Are you communicating with respect, empathy, and purpose? To communicate effectively is to lead with intention, to understand that words have power, that silence has strength, and that true leadership is found not in dominating but in connecting.

To lead like the silverback is to communicate with presence, with purpose, and with restraint. It is to understand that communication is a tool of unity, a means of fostering trust, and a path to collective strength. When we master this art, we become leaders who do not just command but inspire, who do not just instruct but connect. This is the power of communication. This is the essence of leadership.

CHAPTER 8:

TEACHING THROUGH EXAMPLE

Example is not the main thing in influencing others. It is the only thing. —Albert Schweitzer

TEACHING THROUGH EXAMPLE

Leadership is not a position but a practice, not a title but a way of being. True leaders understand that influence is not gained through words alone; it is earned through actions. Teaching through example is the most profound way to lead, a method that transcends instruction and speaks directly to the core of those who follow. To lead by example is to live one's values, to embody principles so deeply that they become evident without need for explanation. In this way, leadership becomes less about directing and more about inspiring—a quiet, persistent influence that shapes others simply through presence and integrity.

In the natural world, the gorilla troop exemplifies this form of leadership. The silverback does not command respect through forceful edicts or constant correction. He leads by living in alignment with the troop's needs, embodying strength, calm, and resilience in every action. His influence is not loud; it is deeply felt. The younger gorillas look to him, observing his every movement, his responses to threats, his interactions with the troop. He does not instruct them with words; he teaches them through example, imparting lessons of courage, patience, and unity through his behavior. His presence is a silent yet powerful guide, shaping the next generation without a single directive.

To teach by example is to embrace a form of leadership that demands self-discipline and authenticity. It is a path that does not allow for shortcuts or pretense. One cannot lead effectively while saying one thing and doing another. Inconsistencies weaken influence, and hollow words fall flat when actions do not align. True leadership is rooted in coherence—the unbroken alignment of words and deeds. When a leader embodies this coherence, they become a beacon, a figure others can look to not because of their title but because of their character.

Reflect on the people who have influenced you most deeply. Were they individuals who merely told you what to do, or were they those who showed you, through their own actions, what is possible? Teaching through example does not rely on authority; it relies on respect, on the willingness to live by the same standards we set for others. Leaders who embody their values inspire loyalty, not because they demand it, but because they have earned it.

In a gorilla troop, the silverback's behavior is a blueprint for others. The younger gorillas do not learn through imposed rules; they learn by observing his responses to life's challenges. When danger looms, the silverback's calm demeanor teaches them resilience. When food is scarce, his patience shows them how to conserve and share. Through these quiet acts, he imparts the values that sustain the troop. His lessons are not explicit, yet they are deeply ingrained, for they are communicated through action rather than instruction.

As leaders, we must ask ourselves: What example are we setting? Do our actions reflect the values we wish to impart, or do we rely on words to fill the gaps left by our inconsistencies? Teaching through example requires a relentless commitment to integrity. It is not about perfection, but about authenticity—about the willingness to live openly, to let our actions speak, even when words would be easier. True influence is born from this commitment, from the courage to embody the principles we wish to see in others.

Leading by example also requires humility. It means recognizing that we are not infallible, that our actions will sometimes fall short of our ideals. But even in these moments, there is an opportunity to teach. When a leader acknowledges their mistakes, they show that strength lies not in perfection but in growth, in the willingness to learn and evolve. The silverback, if challenged, does not respond with brute force but with a steady resolve. He teaches the troop that power is not domination but restraint, that respect is earned through calm confidence rather than aggression.

In our own lives, leading by example means embracing vulnerability. It means being willing to admit when we are wrong, to show that growth is a continual process. When leaders display this humility, they create a culture where others feel safe to do the same. They teach that leadership is not about always having the right answer but about having the courage to seek it. Through this example, they cultivate an environment where people feel empowered to take risks, to learn, and to grow without fear of judgment.

To lead by example is also to understand the power of presence. In the gorilla troop, the silverback's influence is not in his words but in his steady, unwavering presence. His mere proximity brings a sense of security, a reassurance that he is there, that the troop is safe. In leadership, presence is a form of silent guidance, a way to communicate without words. When leaders are present—physically, emotionally, and mentally—they create a foundation of stability. Their presence becomes a source of strength, a reminder that they are fully committed, that they are with their team in both triumph and trial.

Consider the power of presence in your own leadership. Are you truly present with those you lead, or are you distracted, pulled in multiple directions? Presence requires focus, a willingness to set aside distractions and be fully engaged. When leaders show up fully, they send a message of respect. They tell their team, through their actions, that each person matters, that each interaction is valuable. Presence is not just about being physically there; it is about being attentive, about making each person feel seen, heard, and valued.

Teaching through example also means understanding the subtleties of influence. Influence is not something we impose; it is something we cultivate through consistency and authenticity. The silverback does not need to assert his authority constantly; his influence is felt, not forced. In the same way, leaders who teach through example do not rely on coercion or control. Their influence flows naturally from their character, from the trust they inspire, from the respect they earn through their actions.

In modern leadership, influence often becomes a tool to achieve personal goals. But true influence is selfless; it is directed not at gaining personal power but at uplifting others. A leader who teaches through example does not seek to dominate but to empower, to create an environment where each person can thrive. This kind of influence is not about bending others to one's will but about inspiring them to rise to their potential. It is about creating a culture of growth, where each person feels encouraged to develop their own strengths.

Think of the values you wish to instill in those you lead. Are these values reflected in your actions, or are they simply words you speak? Teaching through example requires a level of introspection that many leaders shy away from. It requires us to hold ourselves accountable, to ask if we are living the values we wish to see in others. The silverback does not tell the young gorillas to be strong; he shows them through his presence, through his patience, through his ability to stand firm without unnecessary force.

In times of challenge, teaching through example becomes even more vital. When faced with adversity, a leader's response sets the tone for the entire team. Will we react with fear or with calm? Will we retreat, or will we stand firm? The silverback, when confronted with threats, does not panic. His steadiness becomes the troop's steadiness, his confidence becomes their confidence. In our own lives, we have the same power to shape others through our responses. When we face challenges with resilience, we teach those around us to do the same. When we remain calm, we instill calm in others.

Leadership through example is a powerful tool in conflict resolution as well. In any group, conflicts will arise, and how a leader handles these moments serves as a model for others. The silverback does not engage in petty disputes; he steps back, allowing space for resolution to occur naturally. His restraint teaches the troop that not every issue requires intervention, that not every challenge is a threat. Similarly, leaders who lead by example in conflict show that patience and understanding are often more effective than immediate intervention. They teach that true strength lies in discernment, in knowing when to act and when to let others resolve their own challenges.

Reflect on the conflicts you have faced as a leader. Did you rush to impose a solution, or did you model patience, allowing others to find their way? Teaching through example in conflict is about demonstrating that problems can be solved with respect, that resolution is possible without domination. It is about creating a space where people feel empowered to resolve differences with dignity, guided by the example of a leader who values unity over control.

In the end, teaching through example is the most enduring form of leadership. Words fade, instructions are forgotten, but actions remain. The example we set becomes a legacy, a silent influence that continues even in our absence. The silverback's lessons live on in the troop, shaping each member long after he is gone. His influence is not confined to his physical presence; it is a part of the troop's very fabric, a guide that transcends time.

As you consider your own path in leadership, ask yourself: What example are you leaving behind? Are you teaching through words

TEACHING THROUGH EXAMPLE

alone, or are your actions a testament to your values? To lead through example is to commit to a path of integrity, to walk with a purpose that others can see and follow. It is to understand that our greatest influence comes not from what we say but from who we are.

To lead like a silverback is to embody one's values so fully that they become evident without explanation. It is to live in alignment with purpose, to teach not through direction but through demonstration. This is the power of leading by example. This is the essence of true leadership.

CHAPTER 9:

EMBRACING DIVERSITY

"

It is not our differences that divide us. It is our inability to recognize, accept, and celebrate those differences. —Audre Lorde

EMBRACING DIVERSITY

Diversity is a term that is often spoken of lightly, as though it were an ornament to be added, a token for appearances. But true diversity is not about conforming to superficial standards of inclusion; it is about honoring individuality and strength in difference. Embracing diversity is not a polite exercise but a radical act. It is an acknowledgement that strength does not emerge from uniformity, but from a vibrant array of perspectives, abilities, and experiences. True leaders do not fear difference; they welcome it, knowing that it is diversity that breathes life and resilience into any community.

Look to the gorilla troop for an understanding of this principle in action. Each gorilla, from the powerful silverback to the smallest juvenile, brings a unique role, strength, and perspective to the group. The troop does not seek to make each member identical; it embraces the natural differences, allowing each gorilla to contribute according to its own abilities. The silverback leads not by molding others into his image but by creating a space where each member's distinct traits are valued. He understands that his role is not to force uniformity but to cultivate unity within diversity.

In leadership, embracing diversity means challenging the instinct to control, to impose a single way of being upon others. It requires a willingness to release one's own expectations and to recognize that strength lies not in similarity but in the coexistence of differences. Leaders who demand conformity weaken the potential of their team, suffocating the unique insights and perspectives that only diversity can bring. To lead effectively is not to assemble a team in one's own image, but to allow each person's individuality to flourish within a shared purpose.

Consider your own approach to diversity. Do you genuinely welcome difference, or do you subtly expect others to align with your perspective? True diversity is uncomfortable; it challenges our assumptions, disrupts our habits, and forces us to confront our own limitations. But it is precisely this discomfort that makes diversity powerful. When we surround ourselves with those who are different from us, we are forced to expand, to rethink, to grow beyond the boundaries of our own perspective. Diversity is not merely a value; it is a crucible that strengthens, a force that sharpens and refines.

In a gorilla troop, diversity is not a philosophy; it is a lived reality. Each member has its own instincts, its own role, its own way of contributing to the whole. The mothers protect their young with fierce devotion, the juveniles bring energy and playfulness, the silverback provides strength and stability. Each is essential, each irreplaceable. The troop's resilience is not found in homogeneity but in the intricate balance of differences that form a cohesive whole. Leadership, then, is not about enforcing uniformity but about fostering a space where each individual can contribute fully from their unique place within the group.

As leaders, we must resist the impulse to control, to mold others into our own vision. Embracing diversity means acknowledging that our way is not the only way, that others may bring insights and strengths we cannot see from our own vantage point. This requires humility, the ability to step back and let others bring their full selves to the table. It requires the courage to accept that our perspective, while valuable, is limited, and that our team's strength depends on the breadth of perspectives that each person brings.

Diversity is also a test of resilience. It forces us to confront our biases, to challenge the walls we build around our own identities. A leader who embraces diversity is not only willing to accept difference; they are willing to be changed by it. They see diversity not as a threat to their authority but as an opportunity to expand their understanding, to refine their vision, to grow alongside those they lead. The silverback, for all his strength, does not impose his will upon the troop; he adapts to its needs, respecting each member's role. This adaptability is what makes him a true leader—not a tyrant, but a guide.

Consider the diversity within your own team. Do you view it as an asset, or do you see it as a challenge to be managed? The truth is that diversity is not an asset to be "managed"; it is the raw material from which a dynamic, resilient community is forged. When leaders embrace diversity, they open themselves to a world of ideas, strengths, and perspectives that they could never possess alone. They create a culture where each person feels valued for who they are, not just for what they produce.

In any community, there will be friction—differences in opinion, in approach, in experience. But this friction is not a weakness; it is the spark that fuels growth. The gorilla troop, with all its natural diversity, does not avoid tension; it navigates it with respect. The silverback does not demand blind obedience; he trusts that each member will contribute in their own way, that the differences among them will ultimately strengthen the group. Leaders who embrace this approach create teams that are not only resilient but innovative, teams that do not fear disagreement but see it as a path to discovery.

In leadership, diversity also means accepting that not everyone will follow the same path to the same destination. Some may bring ideas that challenge the status quo, others may bring skills that are unconventional. A leader who embraces diversity is not threatened by this difference; they are inspired by it. They see each individual as a unique source of strength, a voice that adds depth to the chorus. The silverback does not demand that each gorilla mirror his movements; he allows them to find their own rhythm, knowing that their collective strength is greater than the sum of its parts.

This kind of leadership requires a radical openness, a willingness to let go of control. It means allowing others to challenge us, to disrupt our assumptions, to show us new ways of seeing. It is not comfortable; it is not easy. But it is the path to true growth. Leaders who embrace diversity are not content with mere harmony; they seek a deeper unity, one that honors difference as much as it does similarity. They understand that diversity is not a weakness to be overcome but a strength to be celebrated.

Reflect on your own relationship to diversity. Do you genuinely welcome difference, or do you seek to shape it into something familiar? To embrace diversity is to let go of the need for control, to release the expectation that others must see as we see. It is to understand that each person brings something essential to the whole, that our strength lies not in our sameness but in our ability to honor each person's unique perspective.

In the end, diversity is not about conformity; it is about coexistence. It is about creating a space where each individual can thrive, where differences are not suppressed but celebrated. The silverback leads not by demanding uniformity but by fostering unity within diversity. He allows each member of the troop to fulfill their role, to bring their strengths to the whole, to contribute from their place of power. This is the essence of true leadership—not a dominance of the self over others, but a respect for the individual paths that lead to a shared goal.

To lead effectively is to understand that diversity is not an obstacle but an opportunity. It is the raw, unpolished material from which greatness is crafted. When we embrace diversity, we open ourselves to perspectives we could never achieve alone. We create teams that are resilient, adaptable, and deeply connected. We build communities that thrive not in spite of their differences but because of them.

To lead like the silverback is to embrace diversity with strength and humility, to see each person not as a piece to be managed but as an essential part of the whole. It is to understand that our strength lies not in molding others to our vision but in allowing each individual to bring their full self to the collective. This is the power of diversity. This is the path to true unity.

CHAPTER 10:

DEVELOPING FUTURE LEADERS

❝❞

The function of leadership is to produce more leaders, not more followers —Ralph Nader

DEVELOPING FUTURE LEADERS

A leader's legacy is not in the power they hold but in the strength they leave behind. True leadership does not seek to create dependency but independence, to inspire not merely obedience but resilience. A leader's task is to cultivate strength in others, to foster individuals who can stand alone yet choose to stand together. Developing future leaders is not an act of control; it is an act of liberation. It is the process of building minds that think independently, spirits that stand firmly, and characters that grow in the face of challenge.

In the natural order of a gorilla troop, the silverback embodies this approach to leadership. He does not seek to create followers who depend solely on him; he nurtures future leaders within the troop. He teaches through example, showing the younger gorillas how to navigate their world with confidence and respect. His presence provides security, but it does not smother. Each young gorilla is encouraged to find its own strength, its own role, and its own understanding of life within the boundaries of the troop. His guidance is subtle, his influence profound. He develops the future of the troop not by enforcing his will, but by creating an environment where each member can learn to stand strong in their own way.

To develop future leaders is to understand that one's role is not to dictate every step but to provide the ground upon which others can build their own path. This process requires restraint as much as it does guidance. Leaders who feel the need to control every detail, to shape others in their own image, misunderstand the essence of their role. Developing leaders is not about replication; it is about cultivation. It is the ability to see potential where others see rawness, to nurture strength without dictating form, to guide without enforcing conformity.

Consider the young gorillas within the troop. They are not pushed into a mold; they are allowed to explore, to test, to fail. Each failure is a lesson, each challenge a step toward growth. The silverback does not shield them from hardship but watches from a distance, letting them confront their own obstacles. His presence is there when they need it, but it does not overshadow their own experience. This is the essence of developing leaders: allowing others to face difficulty, to learn resilience, and to find their strength not in the absence of struggle but through it.

In leadership, developing future leaders demands a similar approach. It is not about solving every problem for others; it is about empowering them to find their own solutions. Leaders who rush to rescue at every sign of trouble weaken the potential of those they lead. To create leaders, we must give them space to learn, to struggle, to rise on their own. We must resist the urge to impose our solutions and instead encourage them to find their own. It is in this space, in this freedom to confront and overcome, that leaders are born.

Reflect on your own approach to developing others. Do you create followers who look to you for answers, or do you cultivate individuals who can think and act independently? True leadership is not about maintaining authority but about building a foundation upon which others can stand tall. It is about planting seeds that grow beyond your own reach, about fostering autonomy rather than dependence. When we hold too tightly, we stunt the growth of others. But when we let go, when we trust in their potential, we give them the chance to become leaders in their own right.

The silverback's influence within the troop is profound, yet he does not assert it through constant intervention. He observes, he assesses, and he intervenes only when necessary. He understands that to raise strong leaders, one must trust in their ability to find strength on their own. His restraint is not a lack of care; it is the highest form of respect. He respects each member's potential, allowing them to stumble, to learn, to grow. This respect is what forges resilience, what transforms mere followers into future leaders.

In developing leaders, one must also confront the ego. The ego, that desire to be needed, to be central, is a trap that ensnares many leaders. True leadership requires the humility to step back, to know that one's purpose is not to be the center of attention but to empower others to become their own centers of strength. The silverback does not cling to his role; he does not fear the growth of others. He leads with the understanding that his legacy is not his own power, but the strength of those who follow. To develop leaders is to sacrifice one's own need for validation in favor of the growth of others.

In a world that often measures success by personal accolades, this approach to leadership requires a radical shift. To develop future leaders is to focus not on one's own achievements but on the achievements of others. It is to invest in the potential of those around you, to celebrate their growth as a reflection of true leadership. When we look to create leaders, we build a legacy that endures, a strength that goes beyond our own presence.

Developing leaders also means teaching them to embrace challenge rather than avoid it. Many leaders, in their desire to protect, shield others from difficulty. But true leaders understand that struggle is the crucible of growth. In the gorilla troop, the young face their own battles, small but significant moments that test their strength. They are not removed from hardship; they are guided through it. This guidance is subtle yet essential, a presence that reassures without overpowering, that supports without rescuing. The silverback teaches resilience not through words but through the experience he allows others to have.

Consider the challenges faced by those you lead. Do you allow them the space to struggle, to learn resilience, to find their own strength? Or do you intervene at every sign of discomfort, believing that protection is the highest form of care? To develop leaders is to recognize that discomfort is not the enemy; it is a teacher. It is the experiences that test us, that push us beyond our comfort, that reveal our true strength. Leaders who create future leaders do not seek to remove all obstacles; they seek to build individuals who can face them.

To develop future leaders also requires an understanding of timing—knowing when to guide and when to step back. The silverback, for all his strength, does not impose himself constantly; he moves with intention, intervening only when his presence is truly needed. His influence is felt not in constant instruction but in timely action, in moments that shape rather than control. In leadership, this discernment is vital. Leaders who develop others understand that too much intervention stifles growth, while too little leaves others adrift. It is a balance, a dance between support and independence, a rhythm that nurtures leadership without suppressing autonomy.

In developing leaders, one must also teach them the power of self-mastery. To lead others, one must first lead oneself. This is a lesson taught not through words but through example. The silverback's calm presence, his ability to remain composed under pressure, teaches the young gorillas self-control, a discipline that is the foundation of true leadership. In our own lives, we teach self-mastery not by enforcing it upon others but by embodying it. When we demonstrate control, patience, and strength, we show others the path to leading themselves.

Reflect on your own example. Do you embody the qualities you wish to see in future leaders, or do you rely on words alone? Teaching by example is the most powerful way to develop leaders. When others see resilience in our actions, patience in our decisions, and integrity in our character, they learn these qualities not as abstract ideals but as lived realities. True leadership is a mirror; it reflects the qualities we wish to cultivate in others.

Finally, developing future leaders means letting go. It means recognizing that the highest form of leadership is not control but empowerment. When the young gorillas mature, the silverback does not cling to his position out of fear of being replaced. He knows that his legacy is secure not in his own role but in the strength he has fostered in others. Leaders who develop future leaders understand that their purpose is not to be irreplaceable but to make others capable, resilient, and autonomous.

As you reflect on your role in developing others, ask yourself: Are you building individuals who depend on you, or are you nurturing leaders who can stand independently? True leadership is not about creating followers; it is about creating leaders. It is about investing in others, celebrating their growth, and finding fulfillment not in control but in the strength you help them to find within themselves.

To lead like the silverback is to develop leaders who can carry forward the values, strength, and resilience that sustain the group. It is to build a legacy of independence, a community of individuals who are empowered to lead themselves. This is the true purpose of leadership. This is the path to lasting influence.

PART III: THE INNER STRENGTH OF A LEADER

CHAPTER 11:

LEADING WITH COMPASSION

❝❞

The best way to find yourself is to lose yourself in the service of others—Mahatma Gandhi

LEADING WITH COMPASSION

Compassion is often seen as softness, as something that detracts from strength. But true compassion is a force of resilience, a strength that holds others up without seeking validation. To lead with compassion is not to give in to weakness; it is to understand the power of empathy, to see others not as mere instruments but as individuals with their own struggles, strengths, and potential. Compassion is a silent, profound force that builds loyalty and trust, that binds people together in ways that command alone could never achieve.

In a gorilla troop, compassion is a quiet, pervasive strength. The silverback leads with authority, but his authority is tempered by care. He is aware of each member's place, of their needs and vulnerabilities. When a young gorilla stumbles, the silverback's presence reassures rather than rebukes. He does not rush to solve every problem but offers silent support, a presence that communicates safety and trust. His compassion is not a weakness; it is an extension of his strength, a reminder that true leadership seeks to lift others, not dominate them.

In our own lives, leading with compassion demands a similar approach. Compassion in leadership does not mean removing every challenge, nor does it mean ignoring faults. It means recognizing the humanity in others, understanding that each person has their own burdens, their own struggles. Compassion requires patience, empathy, and a willingness to set aside one's own agenda to truly see those we lead. It requires a balance—a strength that knows when to support and when to let others find their own footing.

Reflect on the people you lead. Do you see them only for their roles, or do you recognize their individuality, their unique experiences and challenges? To lead with compassion is to look beyond the surface, to understand the lives behind the roles. It is to value each person not merely for what they can contribute but for who they are. Leaders who show this kind of compassion build communities where people feel seen, valued, and supported. They create spaces where individuals are willing to give their best, not out of fear, but out of trust.

In a gorilla troop, compassion is expressed in simple but powerful ways. The silverback does not dominate constantly; he nurtures connections through gestures of respect and understanding. When tensions arise, he does not escalate conflict but intervenes with calm. His compassion is not a display of weakness; it is a discipline, a strength that holds the group together. In the same way, leaders who embody compassion create an atmosphere of stability, a foundation that withstands challenges because it is built on mutual respect.

Leading with compassion also requires a willingness to listen. Compassion is not a one-sided act; it is a dialogue, a constant engagement with others' perspectives and needs. When leaders listen deeply, they create an environment of trust, a space where people feel safe to express themselves without fear of judgment. Listening is an act of humility; it requires the leader to set aside their own assumptions and to see the world through others' eyes. In this space of genuine listening, compassion grows, and the leader gains insight into the true needs of the team.

Consider the importance of listening in your own leadership. Do you listen to understand, or do you listen to respond? Leaders who listen with compassion do not rush to offer solutions or impose their own views. They create space for others to speak, to be heard. In this act of listening, they demonstrate respect, a recognition of each person's voice and experience. When people feel heard, they become more willing to share openly, to contribute fully. Compassionate listening is a foundation for trust, a bedrock upon which resilient teams are built.

Compassion is also essential in times of hardship. In moments of struggle, compassion is not just a comfort; it is a lifeline, a strength that provides support without diminishing resilience. In the gorilla troop, the silverback does not remove every challenge, but he offers presence. When a member of the troop faces difficulty, he is there, not to rescue but to reassure. His compassion strengthens the troop, reminding each member that they are not alone, that they have a support system around them.

In leadership, compassionate support is a powerful tool. Leaders who respond to hardship with empathy and patience foster an environment where people feel safe to face challenges without fear of rejection. Compassionate leaders do not view struggle as a sign of weakness; they see it as an opportunity for growth. They create spaces where people are encouraged to learn from their experiences, to rise stronger, knowing they have the support of their leader.

To lead with compassion also requires courage. Compassion is not passive; it is an active choice, a decision to put others' well-being at the forefront. It demands a willingness to engage with others' pain, to sit with discomfort without flinching. Compassionate leaders do not shy away from difficult conversations; they approach them with empathy, with a readiness to understand rather than judge. This courage to face others' suffering, to be present in their struggles, is a mark of true strength.

Reflect on your own approach to hardship. Do you offer support without judgment, or do you shy away from others' pain, afraid to confront it? Leading with compassion means standing firm in the face of others' struggles, being a source of strength that does not waver. It is a commitment to be present, to offer support not as a burden but as a gift. This courage to embrace compassion, to offer strength through presence, builds a foundation of trust and loyalty.

In a world that often equates leadership with control, leading with compassion requires a different mindset. Compassion is not about taking over; it is about empowering others to find their own strength. The silverback does not remove every obstacle for the troop; he allows them to face challenges, to grow resilient. His compassion is a quiet strength, a presence that reassures without overshadowing. Leaders who adopt this approach understand that compassion is not an excuse for dependency but a means to foster independence.

In developing compassion, one must also cultivate self-compassion. Leaders who are harsh with themselves, who refuse to acknowledge their own limits, cannot fully embrace compassion for others. Self-compassion is the foundation of compassion for others; it teaches the leader to recognize their own humanity, to accept their own imperfections. When leaders are kind to themselves, they create an environment where others feel safe to do the same. Compassion, then, begins with self-acceptance, with a willingness to treat oneself with the same understanding one would extend to others.

Consider your own relationship with self-compassion. Do you allow yourself the space to grow, to learn, to make mistakes, or do you demand perfection? Leaders who practice self-compassion create a culture of growth, a space where others feel encouraged to strive without fear of failure. They lead by example, showing that strength is not found in harshness but in kindness. When leaders are compassionate with themselves, they inspire others to approach their own challenges with patience and resilience.

To lead with compassion also means recognizing the importance of boundaries. Compassion is not an invitation to be consumed by others' needs; it is a balanced strength that respects both self and others. In the gorilla troop, the silverback provides support without losing his own autonomy. He is present for the troop, but he does not sacrifice his own well-being. In leadership, this balance is essential. Compassion without boundaries leads to burnout; compassion with boundaries becomes a sustainable strength, a steady presence that supports others without losing itself.

Reflect on your own boundaries. Do you offer compassion without sacrificing your own health and well-being? Leaders who balance compassion with boundaries create environments where people feel valued but not entitled to the leader's every moment. They set limits not out of selfishness but out of respect, for themselves and for those they lead. Compassionate boundaries are a strength, a discipline that allows the leader to give fully without depleting their own reserves.

In the end, leading with compassion is not an act of weakness; it is a profound strength, a choice to value others deeply. It is the courage to see others' pain, to be present in their struggles, to support without controlling, and to empower without diminishing. Compassion is the quiet force that builds loyalty, the foundation of trust that endures through both ease and hardship.

To lead like the silverback is to embody this compassion with strength, to create a community where each member feels seen, valued, and supported. It is to understand that leadership is not about elevating oneself but about uplifting others, about building a foundation of trust and respect. This is the power of compassion. This is the essence of true leadership.

CHAPTER 12:

PROTECTING YOUR HOME

❝❞

There is nothing more important than a good, safe, secure home—Rosalynn Carter

A true leader understands that protection is not about mere survival; it is about creating an environment where others feel safe to grow, to thrive, to belong. Protecting one's home is not simply defending against outside threats but guarding the essence of the community—its values, its integrity, its unity. To protect one's home is to act as a steward of the group, to ensure that the people within it feel secure and valued, to preserve the foundation upon which future strength can be built.

In the gorilla troop, the silverback embodies this role with silent vigilance. He does not guard out of fear but out of strength. His presence alone is a reminder to the troop that they are protected, that they are part of something larger than themselves. He watches over his home not merely by warding off threats but by creating a space where each member feels secure, where they can go about their lives without the constant fear of disruption. He protects not only the physical boundaries but the integrity and peace of the community he leads.

In leadership, protecting one's home means more than guarding against visible dangers; it requires safeguarding the very spirit of the community. Leaders who protect their teams do not merely react to external threats; they cultivate an environment that withstands both internal and external pressures. They do not impose control through fear but through consistency, through the trust they inspire, through their unwavering commitment to the group's well-being. To protect one's home is to be the silent guardian, a presence that assures others of their safety without overshadowing their freedom.

PROTECTING YOUR HOME

Reflect on what "home" means within your leadership. Do you see it as merely a physical place, or do you recognize it as a space that holds meaning, that defines identity, that brings people together? Protecting one's home as a leader is not about territory; it is about creating a sanctuary where people feel free to express themselves, to contribute fully, to belong. Leaders who protect their homes guard not only the boundaries but the values that bind the community. They understand that a home is not a place but a feeling, a sense of unity that must be nurtured and defended.

In the gorilla troop, the silverback is ever vigilant, always aware of his surroundings. His protection is not an aggressive display but a calm, watchful presence. When a threat arises, he steps forward, not with unnecessary force but with a strength that reassures the troop. He does not panic; he does not rush. His protection is steady, unwavering, a reminder to the group that they are safe. In the same way, leaders protect their teams not by creating an atmosphere of constant vigilance but by instilling a sense of confidence, a quiet assurance that they are there to stand against any threat.

Protecting one's home also means protecting its integrity. It is not enough to guard against external threats; a leader must also be willing to confront internal challenges, to address issues that could weaken the unity of the group. This requires courage, a willingness to hold others accountable, and the strength to make difficult decisions when necessary. The silverback, though calm, does not tolerate disruption within the troop. He intervenes when necessary, setting boundaries that preserve harmony. His protection is not passive; it is an active commitment to maintaining the peace and unity of the group.

In leadership, this form of protection requires discernment. Not every challenge demands intervention, but some require it. Leaders who protect their teams understand when to step forward and when to hold back. They do not avoid conflict; they address it with purpose, with the understanding that unchecked tensions can erode the group from within. Protecting one's home is a responsibility that requires strength tempered by wisdom, action guided by restraint. It is the mark of a leader who understands that preservation is not passive but active, a choice to guard what matters most.

Consider the threats that face your own "home" as a leader. Are they external forces, or do they come from within? Are they visible challenges, or are they subtle forces that undermine unity? True leaders are not only protectors against visible dangers but guardians of the unseen, vigilant against complacency, misunderstanding, and erosion of values. They do not allow minor conflicts to fester, nor do they ignore the quiet discontent that can fracture unity. Instead, they create a culture of openness, a space where issues can be addressed directly, a home that stands firm against both seen and unseen threats.

Protecting one's home also means building resilience within the community. A leader's role is not only to defend but to strengthen, to create a foundation that can withstand storms. The silverback does not shield the troop from every challenge; he allows them to experience hardship, to grow resilient. His protection is not about removing all obstacles but about preparing the group to face them. In the same way, leaders who protect their teams empower others to stand strong, to develop the skills and resilience that will sustain them. They do not create dependency but independence, a strength that does not waver when faced with difficulty.

Reflect on how you approach resilience within your own team. Do you shield them from every hardship, or do you allow them to grow through experience? To protect one's home is not to remove every challenge but to equip others to face them. Leaders who build resilient teams create communities that are not only safe but strong, communities that can withstand trials without collapsing. This resilience is the true strength of a home, a foundation that sustains not only through ease but through adversity.

In protecting one's home, one must also protect its spirit. The silverback does not simply guard the physical space of the troop; he guards its identity, its way of life. He protects the bonds that hold them together, the shared experiences that define them. In leadership, protecting the spirit of the group means preserving its culture, its values, its shared purpose. It means understanding that a home is not a physical structure but a network of relationships, a community bound by trust and mutual respect. Leaders who protect this spirit create communities that endure, that thrive not only in good times but in all times.

Consider the culture of your own "home." Do you nurture it, or do you allow it to be eroded by external pressures? Protecting one's home is about preserving the essence of the group, the qualities that make it unique. It is a commitment to defend not only against external threats but against anything that would weaken the unity and identity of the community. Leaders who protect their homes hold fast to the values that define the group, creating a sanctuary that stands firm in the face of change.

Finally, protecting one's home means preparing for a future beyond oneself. The silverback leads with the knowledge that his role is temporary, that his protection must prepare the troop to endure in his absence. He does not cling to power; he empowers others to carry forward his legacy. True protection is not about control; it is about stewardship, a commitment to creating a home that will stand strong even after one's departure. Leaders who protect their teams with this mindset create a legacy that endures, a strength that outlasts their own presence.

Reflect on your own legacy. Are you building a home that will endure, or are you focused only on immediate protection? Leaders who think beyond the present create communities that are resilient, communities that stand firm not because of one person but because of the collective strength that has been nurtured. Protecting one's home is not about building walls; it is about building foundations, creating a strength that endures through time.

PROTECTING YOUR HOME

To protect like the silverback is to lead with quiet strength, to guard not only against visible threats but against anything that would diminish the group's integrity. It is to understand that leadership is a role of stewardship, a commitment to safeguard the values, the unity, and the strength of the community. This is the power of protecting one's home. This is the essence of true leadership.

CHAPTER 13:

THE POWER OF PLAY

" "

It is a happy talent to know how to play
—*Ralph Waldo Emerson*

THE POWER OF PLAY

Play is often viewed as a luxury, something to be enjoyed in moments of ease and discarded in times of purpose. But to think of play merely as recreation is to miss its profound significance. True play is not an escape from reality; it is an engagement with it. Play fosters resilience, innovation, and connection. It is an activity that allows individuals to explore, to test limits, to experiment without fear. In leadership, play is not a distraction; it is a powerful tool for growth and connection, a way to create an environment where creativity and camaraderie thrive.

In a gorilla troop, play is woven into the very fabric of daily life. The young gorillas wrestle, chase, and tumble with a boundless joy that strengthens not only their bodies but their minds. Through play, they develop the skills and instincts they will need to navigate their environment. They learn balance, agility, and confidence, preparing themselves for the challenges they will one day face. Play within the troop is not a trivial pursuit; it is a means of survival, a training ground that builds resilience and adaptability. Even the silverback participates at times, joining the younger members in moments of lighthearted interaction, showing them that strength does not always require rigidity.

In leadership, the power of play is often overlooked. We tend to value discipline, focus, and efficiency, forgetting that creativity and resilience are born in spaces of freedom. Play allows the mind to wander, to test ideas, to explore possibilities that rigid discipline might overlook. Leaders who embrace play within their teams create an environment that encourages curiosity, that fosters a sense of adventure, that inspires innovation. When people are given permission to play, they engage with their work in new ways, discovering solutions and insights that would otherwise remain hidden.

Consider the culture within your own leadership. Do you create space for play, or is it stifled by relentless focus? True play requires a freedom of thought, a willingness to step outside conventional boundaries and to engage with the world from a place of curiosity. Leaders who cultivate play understand that it is not a waste of time; it is an investment in mental flexibility, a way to build a team that can think on its feet, adapt to change, and approach challenges with an open mind. Play is the birthplace of resilience, a training ground that prepares people to face the unexpected with confidence.

In the gorilla troop, play also serves as a way to strengthen social bonds. Through shared moments of joy and laughter, the young gorillas form connections that will carry them through their lives. These bonds are not built through discipline alone but through the lightness of shared experience, the trust that comes from letting down guards and engaging fully in the moment. Play creates a space where hierarchies dissolve, where connection is forged through presence rather than position. The silverback, though respected and revered, does not abstain from these moments; he joins them, reinforcing the unity of the group through shared play.

As leaders, we must recognize the role of play in building relationships. Play is a bridge, a way to connect with others that transcends roles and titles. When leaders participate in play, they show that they are not distant figures but integral members of the team. They build rapport, foster trust, and create an environment where people feel safe to be themselves. Play breaks down barriers, allowing people to see each other beyond their roles, to connect as individuals united not just by purpose but by shared joy.

Reflect on your own relationships within your team. Are they built solely on structure, or do they include moments of genuine connection? Leaders who embrace play create a culture where people feel valued not only for their work but for who they are. They show that leadership is not merely about productivity but about building a community where each person feels connected, where bonds are strengthened through shared moments of laughter and lightness. Play is a reminder that strength is found not in constant seriousness but in the ability to balance purpose with joy.

Play also fosters innovation. In play, the mind is free to explore without fear of failure, to test ideas without the constraints of immediate results. In the gorilla troop, play is a time of experimentation, a way for the young to learn what their bodies and minds are capable of. They push limits, they explore, they adapt. This willingness to engage with the unknown, to explore without fear, is what ultimately prepares them for the challenges of adulthood. Leaders who encourage play within their teams foster a similar spirit of exploration. They create an environment where people feel free to innovate, to test ideas, to think creatively without the pressure of immediate success.

Consider the approach to innovation within your own team. Is creativity encouraged, or is it stifled by the demand for predictable results? Leaders who value play understand that creativity requires freedom, a space where ideas can emerge naturally, where failure is seen not as a setback but as a stepping stone. Play cultivates a mindset of possibility, a willingness to explore the unknown, a readiness to embrace the new. When leaders make space for play, they make space for growth, for ideas that push boundaries, for solutions that are as bold as they are effective.

In times of difficulty, the power of play becomes even more evident. Play is not just a form of relaxation; it is a source of resilience. In the gorilla troop, even during times of stress, play remains a part of their lives. It is a way to release tension, to reaffirm bonds, to find strength in joy. The silverback allows these moments, understanding that play is not a distraction but a necessity, a means of reinforcing the group's unity and resilience. When leaders encourage play during times of hardship, they provide their teams with a way to cope, to find lightness in the face of challenge, to remember that resilience is as much a mental state as it is a physical one.

Reflect on your own approach to adversity. Do you allow space for moments of play, or do you demand constant seriousness? Leaders who understand the power of play do not deny the reality of difficulty; they simply offer a way to navigate it with balance. They recognize that resilience is strengthened through joy, that play provides a release, a reminder that hardship does not define the whole of existence. When leaders make room for play, they help their teams approach challenges with a sense of calm, a confidence that they can face adversity without losing sight of joy.

Play also brings with it a sense of perspective. It reminds us that life is not only about achieving goals but about experiencing it fully. In the gorilla troop, play is a way to live fully in the present, to engage with life not only through survival but through moments of lightheartedness and freedom. The young gorillas do not play out of necessity; they play because it is part of what it means to be alive. Leaders who embrace play bring this perspective to their teams, showing that work is not merely about output but about engagement, that life is richer when we allow ourselves to experience it with a sense of joy.

As a leader, consider the role of perspective in your approach. Do you see play as a waste of time, or do you recognize it as an essential part of a balanced life? Leaders who value play understand that it is not an escape but a celebration, a way to engage with the present, to find meaning beyond achievement. Play brings a sense of balance, a reminder that success is not only about what we accomplish but about how fully we engage with life itself.

In the end, the power of play lies in its ability to bring people together, to foster creativity, to build resilience, and to deepen connection. Play is not a distraction from purpose; it is an expression of it. When leaders embrace play, they create environments where people feel free to express themselves, to explore, to connect, and to grow. They build teams that are not only strong but adaptable, not only focused but engaged. Play is a reminder that strength is found not in constant rigidity but in the flexibility to embrace both work and joy.

To lead like the silverback is to recognize the value of play, to understand that true strength is balanced by lightness, that resilience is built not only through discipline but through joy. It is to create a community where play is seen not as a luxury but as a necessity, where people are encouraged to connect, to experiment, and to find strength in shared laughter. This is the power of play. This is the essence of a truly resilient, creative, and united community.

CHAPTER 14:

FACING CHALLENGES TOGETHER

""

Alone we can do so little; together we can do so much —Helen Keller

Challenges are inevitable, a constant in the lives of both individuals and communities. But it is not the presence of adversity that defines a group; it is how they face it. To confront challenges together is to find strength in unity, to embrace the power that emerges when individuals stand side by side, supporting one another. True leadership understands that resilience is not an isolated trait but a collective force. A leader's role is not only to face challenges but to rally others, to cultivate a community where each person feels the weight of adversity lifted by shared purpose and mutual support.

In a gorilla troop, survival depends on this sense of togetherness. The silverback stands at the forefront, vigilant and ready, but he is not alone in his role as protector. The mothers, the juveniles, even the younger males, all have a role to play in the troop's defense. When danger approaches, each member knows their place, understands the part they play in preserving the group. They do not scatter; they gather, uniting under the shared instinct to protect one another. This collective strength is not born from hierarchy alone but from loyalty, from a sense of belonging that binds them together in both times of peace and moments of threat.

As leaders, we must learn to cultivate this same unity within our own teams. Facing challenges together requires more than mere cooperation; it demands a commitment to each other's well-being, a willingness to stand firm in the face of adversity. Leaders who foster this environment do not simply demand loyalty; they inspire it through example, through their own willingness to share in the struggle, to

FACING CHALLENGES TOGETHER

bear the weight alongside others. When people feel that their leader stands with them, they become more willing to stand together, to face challenges not as isolated individuals but as a united force.

Consider the challenges your team faces. Do you create an environment where people feel connected, where they trust that they can rely on one another? True unity is not created by commands; it is forged through shared experience, through the quiet resilience that emerges when people know they are not alone. Leaders who understand this create teams that do not fracture under pressure but draw closer, finding strength not in isolation but in collective effort. Facing challenges together is not about protecting oneself alone; it is about building a foundation of trust, a shared purpose that strengthens with every adversity.

In a gorilla troop, facing challenges together also means understanding each other's strengths and weaknesses. Each gorilla contributes to the group in their own way, and the silverback does not expect each member to react in the same manner. Some are naturally bolder, others are more cautious; each brings something unique to the group. The silverback's role is to recognize these differences, to channel them into a collective strength. As leaders, we must do the same. True unity does not erase individuality; it honors it, using each person's unique strengths to face challenges more effectively.

Reflect on your own team. Do you see each person for their individual strengths, or do you expect uniformity in response?

Leaders who face challenges with their teams understand that diversity in approach is a source of resilience. When each person feels valued for who they are, they bring their full selves to the effort, contributing not only their skills but their loyalty. Facing challenges together requires a leader to embrace this diversity, to see it not as a hindrance but as the very foundation of strength.

Facing challenges together also demands vulnerability. To confront adversity as a group, each person must feel safe to express their concerns, their fears, their limitations. In the gorilla troop, even the silverback, though powerful, does not pretend to be invincible. His presence reassures, but his openness to the group's support fosters trust. He does not isolate himself; he includes others in the struggle. This willingness to be part of the collective effort, to rely on others as much as they rely on him, creates a culture of mutual support.

As leaders, vulnerability can feel like a risk, an exposure of weakness. But in reality, vulnerability builds trust; it shows that no one is above the shared experience, that each person has a place in the struggle. Leaders who embrace vulnerability allow others to step forward, to contribute their strengths in times of need. They create a culture where people are willing to support one another, knowing that no one stands alone. This mutual support is the true essence of unity, a force that does not waver under pressure but grows stronger.

In times of challenge, the power of communication becomes even more essential. In the gorilla troop, communication is clear and instinctive. A glance, a gesture, a vocalization—all serve to convey

FACING CHALLENGES TOGETHER

intention, to coordinate the group's response. There is no chaos; each member understands their role, responding as part of the whole. In leadership, communication is the lifeline that keeps the group connected, ensuring that each person understands the direction, the purpose, and the role they play. Leaders who communicate openly foster a sense of clarity, a shared understanding that aligns the group in moments of challenge.

Consider your approach to communication in times of adversity. Do you provide direction, clarity, and purpose, or do you leave people to navigate challenges in isolation? Leaders who face challenges with their teams communicate consistently, offering reassurance and direction. They do not leave others in the dark but provide the light that guides the group through difficulty. Communication in times of challenge is not about control; it is about creating alignment, ensuring that each person feels part of the whole, united in purpose.

In facing challenges together, a sense of shared ownership is also essential. The gorilla troop does not rely solely on the silverback for survival; each member takes responsibility, contributing to the safety and success of the group. This shared ownership creates a community where each individual feels invested, where the success of one is the success of all. Leaders who foster this sense of ownership build teams where people are willing to give their best, where loyalty is not forced but freely offered. Shared ownership is the foundation of true unity, a bond that ensures each person feels a part of the group's success.

Reflect on the sense of ownership within your own team. Do people feel connected to the collective outcome, or do they see challenges as problems for someone else to solve? Leaders who inspire ownership create communities that are resilient, where each person takes pride in the group's success. Facing challenges together is not about reliance on a single leader; it is about creating a network of support, a community where each person feels accountable, valued, and essential.

Facing challenges together also means celebrating resilience. In the gorilla troop, every shared experience, every moment of unity strengthens the group. They do not dwell on fear; they learn, adapt, and move forward with renewed strength. In leadership, this celebration of resilience is vital. Leaders who recognize and celebrate the team's ability to overcome challenges create a culture of strength, a space where people feel empowered by their own resilience. They show that challenges are not to be feared but embraced, that every difficulty is an opportunity to grow stronger together.

Consider how you acknowledge resilience within your team. Do you recognize the strength it takes to face adversity, or do you overlook it in pursuit of the next goal? Leaders who celebrate resilience build confidence, showing the team that they are capable, that they have faced challenges and will face them again. This celebration of resilience is not mere praise; it is a reminder that strength is found in unity, that the team's ability to stand together is its greatest asset.

FACING CHALLENGES TOGETHER

In the end, facing challenges together is about building a foundation of trust, loyalty, and shared strength. The gorilla troop does not fear adversity because they know they face it as one, united by bonds that go beyond mere survival. As leaders, our role is to cultivate this unity, to inspire a loyalty that endures, a resilience that does not falter. To face challenges together is to embrace the power of community, to understand that true strength is found not in isolation but in the unwavering support of others.

To lead like the silverback is to create a community where each person feels valued, where challenges are met not with fear but with resolve. It is to build a team that does not stand alone but stands together, finding strength in unity, courage in connection, and resilience in shared purpose. This is the power of facing challenges together. This is the essence of a truly united and resilient community.

CHAPTER 15:

STRENGTH IN STILLNESS

❝❞

In stillness the mind escapes from the influence of external things and finds itself, undisturbed, and in that stillness there is strength
—*Marcus Aurelius*

STRENGTH IN STILLNESS

In a world that celebrates action, movement, and constant progress, stillness is often misunderstood. Yet true strength is not always found in motion; it is born in the quiet, in the moments of calm when one gathers focus, clarity, and resolve. Strength in stillness is not passive; it is deliberate, intentional, and disciplined. To lead effectively, one must understand the power of restraint, the quiet force that comes not from action alone but from the ability to be still, to observe, to allow insight to emerge without forcing it.

In a gorilla troop, the silverback embodies this strength in stillness. His power is not displayed through constant activity but through his steady presence. He does not dominate through endless movement; he commands respect through the calm assurance of his stance. He does not react to every disturbance, nor does he rush to assert his authority. Instead, he stands watchful, embodying a presence that reassures the troop and signals that all is well. His stillness is not a lack of action; it is a purposeful calm, a silent strength that allows him to respond with clarity when needed.

As leaders, we must learn to cultivate this strength in stillness. In the rush to accomplish and achieve, it is easy to overlook the power of quiet presence, the resilience found in moments of reflection. Strength in stillness is the discipline to pause, to gather one's thoughts before acting, to center oneself amid the noise. Leaders who embrace stillness create a space where focus can flourish, where decisions are not made in haste but are the result of clear, intentional thought. In stillness, there is a grounding force, a foundation upon which true strength is built.

Reflect on your own approach to leadership. Do you allow yourself moments of stillness, or are you caught in the cycle of constant activity? Leaders who cultivate stillness understand that true power does not come from relentless action but from the clarity gained in moments of pause. When we embrace stillness, we create a foundation that supports intentional action. We move not out of compulsion but out of choice, directed by a deeper understanding rather than reactive impulse.

In the gorilla troop, stillness also serves as a means of conserving energy. The silverback does not waste his strength on unnecessary displays of dominance or activity. He moves with purpose, using his energy only when required, preserving his strength for moments of true need. This economy of movement, this restraint, is a lesson in efficiency. As leaders, we must recognize that constant activity is not a sign of productivity. Strength lies in knowing when to act and when to wait, in the patience to conserve energy until the moment calls for it.

Consider the value of restraint in your own life. Do you feel compelled to react to every situation, or do you allow yourself the space to respond intentionally? Leaders who understand the power of stillness do not rush to impose themselves on every situation. They practice restraint, understanding that some challenges resolve themselves, that wisdom often emerges in the quiet moments between action and reaction. By conserving energy, by acting only when necessary, they maintain a reserve of strength that can be drawn upon when it matters most.

Stillness also fosters clarity. In the noise of constant movement, clarity is often the first casualty. The mind, overwhelmed by distraction, loses its focus, its ability to see with precision. But in stillness, the mind finds its center. In the gorilla troop, the silverback's calm allows him to observe his surroundings with a clarity that others might miss. He sees not only what is but what could be, his vision unclouded by haste. In leadership, this clarity is essential. Leaders who embrace stillness develop the ability to see beyond immediate concerns, to gain a broader perspective that guides them through complexity.

Reflect on the clarity in your own leadership. Do you allow yourself moments to step back, to view challenges from a distance, or are you constantly immersed in the details? Leaders who cultivate stillness see with greater depth. They do not rush to judgment but allow insight to emerge naturally, giving themselves the space to understand fully before they act. In this clarity, they find the wisdom to make decisions that are grounded, thoughtful, and far-reaching.

In moments of stillness, there is also space for self-reflection. To lead others, one must first lead oneself, and this requires a willingness to look inward. The silverback, in his calm moments, is not only watching over his troop but reflecting on his own role within it. This self-awareness, this introspective strength, is the foundation of effective leadership. Leaders who embrace stillness cultivate a deeper understanding of themselves—their strengths, their limitations, their motivations. They lead not from ego but from a place of self-mastery, a place where actions are aligned with purpose.

Consider your own practice of self-reflection. Do you give yourself the time to understand your own motivations, or do you move without questioning? Leaders who take time for stillness develop a greater sense of alignment, a consistency between their values and their actions. They lead with authenticity because they know themselves, because they have taken the time to explore their own inner landscape. In this self-awareness, they find a strength that is unshakable, a resilience that is rooted in clarity and purpose.

Strength in stillness is also a form of resilience. In the face of adversity, the impulse is often to act, to react, to solve immediately. But stillness teaches us that not every problem requires immediate resolution. Sometimes, strength is found in waiting, in allowing the challenge to unfold, in trusting that clarity will emerge with time. The silverback does not rush to confront every minor disturbance; he waits, observing, discerning whether intervention is truly necessary. His stillness is not a lack of concern; it is a confidence, a resilience that trusts in his ability to respond effectively when the moment demands.

Reflect on your response to adversity. Do you act out of urgency, or do you allow yourself the patience to wait, to see with clarity before you respond? Leaders who embrace stillness develop a resilience that does not waver under pressure. They understand that strength is not always in the immediate reaction but in the patience to hold steady, in the courage to wait until the right course becomes clear. In this stillness, they find a strength that is calm, enduring, and unshakeable.

Stillness is also a source of connection. In a gorilla troop, the silverback's calm presence is a grounding force for the others. His stillness reassures them, allowing each member to feel safe and focused. In leadership, a calm presence has the same effect. Leaders who are grounded in stillness create a sense of stability for their teams. They are not pulled by every whim or crisis; they remain centered, a source of strength that others can rely on. In this stillness, they cultivate trust, showing that they are not reactive but thoughtful, not impulsive but intentional.

Consider the effect of your own presence on those you lead. Do you offer a calm, grounded influence, or do you contribute to the rush and urgency? Leaders who embrace stillness create environments where people feel secure, where challenges are met with focus rather than panic. Their strength is a source of stability, a reminder that calmness is not a lack of action but a power in itself. In stillness, they find the foundation upon which their team's resilience is built.

In the end, strength in stillness is about mastering oneself, about cultivating a presence that does not seek validation through constant activity but finds power in quiet focus. To lead with stillness is to understand that resilience is not merely physical; it is mental, emotional, and spiritual. It is the ability to hold steady, to move only when movement is required, to act from a place of deep conviction rather than restless energy.

To lead like the silverback is to embrace the strength found in stillness, to create a space where calm prevails over chaos, where clarity guides action, and where resilience is built not through force but through quiet focus. This is the power of stillness. This is the essence of a truly centered and resilient leader.

PART IV: PRACTICES FOR A BALANCED LIFE

CHAPTER 16:

THE VALUE OF SILENCE

" "

Silence is the sleep that nourishes wisdom
—Francis Bacon

Silence is often misunderstood as emptiness, a void to be filled with words, action, or distraction. Yet silence, when embraced, is far from empty. True silence is full of potential, a space that holds strength, reflection, and insight. It is a powerful tool, a source of clarity that strips away the noise of ego, assumption, and impulse, allowing leaders to connect with deeper truths. To understand the value of silence is to recognize that not all wisdom is spoken, that some insights are only found in the quiet spaces within ourselves.

In the life of a gorilla troop, silence plays an essential role. The silverback, though a figure of strength and authority, does not constantly assert his presence through noise or display. He communicates much through his silent gaze, his watchful demeanor, his calm. In moments of silence, he observes, taking in the subtleties of his surroundings, listening to what cannot be heard in words. His silence is not an absence of leadership; it is an embodiment of it. Through his quiet, he commands respect and cultivates a sense of stability for the troop.

As leaders, we must learn to appreciate the value of silence in a world that often glorifies constant communication, immediate responses, and a flood of information. Silence is not an admission of uncertainty; it is a conscious choice, an act of restraint that allows for deeper understanding. Leaders who embrace silence create a space where thoughts can settle, where impulses are tempered, and where true clarity emerges. In silence, there is strength—a quiet force that brings balance and depth to leadership.

Reflect on your own relationship with silence. Do you fill it with words, actions, or distractions, or do you allow yourself to sit with it, to listen beyond the immediate noise? Leaders who cultivate silence understand that it is a space of growth, a moment to gather strength and insight. Silence allows us to see beyond the surface, to connect with the heart of the matter without the interference of ego or fear. In silence, we find the foundation upon which thoughtful leadership is built.

In a gorilla troop, silence is also a means of communication. The silverback's silence is often more powerful than words. His quiet presence signals calm, authority, and confidence to the group. He does not need to dominate with noise; his silence speaks of control, of strength contained and ready, of a presence that reassures without overwhelming. When danger approaches, his silence does not convey fear but a calculated calm, a watchfulness that tells the troop to remain focused, to trust in his guidance. His silence is not passive; it is intentional, a choice that reflects his mastery over his own reactions and emotions.

As leaders, we can learn from this example. Silence in leadership is not a retreat from communication but an elevated form of it. When we are silent, we give others space to think, to express, to bring forth their own insights. Leaders who embrace silence communicate that they do not need to fill every moment with their own thoughts; they trust the process, trust the power of presence. Silence allows others to be heard, fostering an environment where ideas emerge freely, where individuals feel valued for their own voices rather than overshadowed by a leader's constant input.

Consider the role of silence in your own leadership. Do you allow silence to exist in conversations, or do you feel compelled to fill every pause with guidance or instruction? Leaders who understand the value of silence recognize that it is a gift, a space that allows others to speak from their true selves, to bring forth ideas and perspectives that might otherwise remain hidden. In silence, we give people room to think, to reflect, to contribute meaningfully. Silence, then, becomes a tool of empowerment, a reminder that leadership is not about dominating the conversation but about inviting others into it.

Silence is also a source of reflection. In a world that rewards immediate reactions and fast-paced decision-making, silence offers a chance to pause, to consider fully before acting. The silverback does not rush to respond to every noise or movement; he observes, he assesses, he chooses his actions carefully. His silence allows him to gather information, to understand his environment deeply before intervening. As leaders, we must learn to use silence in the same way. Silence is an opportunity for reflection, a moment to align our actions with our values, to ensure that each choice is guided not by impulse but by clarity and purpose.

Reflect on your own decision-making process. Do you allow yourself moments of silence, of genuine pause, or do you feel pressured to respond instantly? Leaders who embrace silence develop a discipline of reflection, a practice that ensures each action is grounded in intention. Silence creates space for wisdom, allowing us to see beyond immediate concerns, to understand the broader implications of our choices. In silence, we find the clarity that enables us to act not from haste but from conviction.

In times of conflict, silence is an invaluable tool. The impulse to react, to assert, to correct can be strong, but silence allows us to rise above reaction, to approach the situation with calm and control. In the gorilla troop, when tension arises, the silverback often responds with silence. He does not escalate; he holds his ground, observing without unnecessary intervention. His silence communicates a powerful message: that strength does not lie in volume, that leadership does not require constant assertion. His silence diffuses tension, creating space for resolution rather than conflict.

As leaders, silence in moments of tension requires a kind of strength that transcends words. Silence does not avoid conflict; it approaches it with patience, with a focus on understanding rather than control. Leaders who respond to conflict with silence offer a path to resolution that is based on reflection, on empathy, on listening. In silence, we communicate that we are open to understanding, that we value the process of resolution more than the immediacy of reaction. This silent strength creates an atmosphere where conflict can be addressed with respect, where differences are not magnified but bridged.

Consider how you handle tension within your team. Do you respond with silence, allowing space for reflection, or do you react immediately, fueling the urgency of the moment? Leaders who understand the value of silence in conflict create an environment where people feel safe to express themselves, where issues can be resolved thoughtfully. Silence is a reminder that resolution is not found in force but in patience, in the calm presence that guides rather than controls.

Silence is also a path to self-awareness. In the quiet, away from the demands of others, we come face to face with ourselves. The silverback, in his moments of silence, is not only observing his surroundings but connecting with his own instincts, his own presence. This self-connection, this inner stillness, is the foundation of his leadership. Leaders who cultivate silence allow themselves the time to explore their own thoughts, their own motivations. In silence, they confront their own strengths and limitations, their own fears and desires. This self-awareness is the foundation of authentic leadership, a strength that is unshakable because it is grounded in truth.

Reflect on your own practice of self-awareness. Do you create moments of silence to connect with your own thoughts, or do you lose yourself in the noise of constant activity? Leaders who embrace silence cultivate a relationship with themselves, a foundation of self-knowledge that guides their actions. In silence, they confront their own fears, their own biases, their own values. This inner strength, this self-mastery, is what enables them to lead from a place of authenticity, a place where actions and words are aligned.

Silence also allows us to connect more deeply with others. In a world filled with endless noise, silence is a rare gift, an invitation to listen fully, to engage meaningfully. The silverback's silence is not isolation; it is a space where others feel his presence without feeling overwhelmed by it. His silence allows each member of the troop to feel seen, valued, understood. As leaders, our silence can serve the same purpose. Silence is not withdrawal; it is a conscious choice to listen, to make space for others' voices, to connect with them in a way that words alone cannot achieve.

Consider the way you connect with others in your team. Do you give them the gift of silence, or do you fill every moment with guidance, instruction, or opinion? Leaders who understand the value of silence offer their teams a presence that is steady, attentive, and open. In silence, they communicate that they are fully present, that they are not merely listening to respond but listening to understand. Silence deepens connection, fostering relationships that are not built on noise but on genuine engagement.

In leadership, silence is ultimately a source of power. It is the ability to hold space, to guide without force, to lead without overwhelming. The silverback's silence is a reminder that true power does not need to be constantly expressed; it is felt, sensed, understood. Leaders who cultivate silence develop an inner strength that does not depend on external validation, a resilience that is grounded in self-mastery. They lead with calm, with clarity, with an authority that does not need to announce itself.

In the end, the value of silence lies in its ability to connect us with ourselves, with others, and with the deeper truths that can only be heard in the quiet. Silence is not emptiness; it is fullness, a space where insight, strength, and understanding can emerge. To lead with silence is to lead with wisdom, to create a space where others feel safe, where clarity reigns, where strength is found not in noise but in calm.

To lead like the silverback is to understand the power of silence, to know that true strength is not found in constant assertion but in the quiet presence that speaks of resilience, clarity, and inner mastery. This is the value of silence. This is the essence of a wise and centered leader.

CHAPTER 17:

INSTINCTS AND INTUITION

❝❞

Trust yourself. You know more than you think you do —Benjamin Spock

LIVE AND LEAD LIKE A GORILLA

In a world that often idolizes logic, analysis, and structure, instinct and intuition are qualities that can seem primitive, almost unfashionable. Yet, some of the greatest wisdom lies within these silent guides, an inner knowing that goes beyond the rational mind, an awareness that cannot be measured but is deeply felt. To lead effectively, one must learn to trust these inner currents—to recognize the voice of intuition, the pulse of instinct, as legitimate sources of wisdom. Instincts and intuition are not opposing forces to logic; they are its companions, sources of insight that, when combined with reason, lead to profound clarity and depth.

In a gorilla troop, survival depends on instinct. The silverback does not analyze every movement within the troop, nor does he question every sound from the forest. He operates from a place of deep awareness, an instinctual understanding of his surroundings, his troop, and himself. His instincts guide him, helping him sense potential threats before they appear, guiding his actions with a confidence that cannot be taught or measured. This instinctual wisdom is the foundation of his leadership, a strength that is not calculated but deeply felt.

As leaders, we, too, must learn to honor the role of instinct and intuition. It is easy to ignore these silent guides, to dismiss them in favor of visible data or tangible evidence. Yet instinct and intuition, when trusted, bring a kind of wisdom that logic alone cannot provide. They guide us toward insights that lie beneath the surface, offering perspectives that are subtle, nuanced, and invaluable.

INSTINCTS AND INTUITION

Leaders who trust their intuition make decisions with a confidence that is grounded not only in reason but in a deep connection to their own inner knowing.

Reflect on your relationship with your own instincts. Do you listen to them, or do you silence them in favor of external evidence? Leaders who embrace intuition understand that it is not an impulsive force; it is a cultivated skill, a quiet sense that grows stronger the more it is trusted. In a world of constant information, intuition becomes a compass, guiding us toward the truths that lie beyond the noise. Trusting one's instincts is an act of self-respect, an acknowledgment that there is wisdom within us that transcends analysis.

Instinct and intuition are also essential in times of uncertainty. In the face of unknowns, logic can falter, caught in a loop of hypotheticals and projections. But intuition sees through the fog; it senses patterns, makes connections, grasps possibilities that are invisible to reason. The silverback, when confronted with an unfamiliar sound or sight, does not freeze in analysis; he trusts his instinct. His body, his senses, his mind—each part of him is tuned to respond without hesitation. This instinctual confidence is not recklessness; it is the product of experience, of deep awareness, of trust in himself.

As leaders, we must cultivate this instinctual confidence. In times of uncertainty, intuition provides a path forward, a sense of direction that does not rely on external validation. Leaders who trust their intuition in uncertain moments project a calm confidence, a strength that reassures others. Their decisions are not swayed by doubt but guided by an inner clarity, a sense of knowing that transcends visible evidence. In this trust of intuition, leaders find resilience, a grounded confidence that others can rely upon.

Consider your response to uncertainty. Do you trust your intuition, or do you seek constant validation from others? Leaders who honor their instincts create a foundation of strength, a sense of being grounded that comes from within. This self-trust radiates, inspiring others to find their own confidence, to trust in their own intuition. Intuition in leadership is not only a personal tool; it is a force that strengthens the entire team, creating an environment where people feel empowered to trust their own inner wisdom.

Instincts and intuition are also deeply connected to empathy. Intuition allows leaders to sense the unspoken, to understand emotions and dynamics that are not explicitly expressed. In a gorilla troop, the silverback's instincts help him read the needs of his troop, sensing tension, fear, or unease without words. His actions are guided not only by observation but by a felt understanding of the group's emotional landscape. This intuitive empathy creates a foundation of trust, a sense that each member's unspoken needs are acknowledged and respected.

As leaders, this intuitive empathy is invaluable. It allows us to connect with others on a deeper level, to understand their perspectives, to sense their needs without requiring explicit communication. Leaders who cultivate this intuition are able to lead with compassion, responding not only to visible needs but to the subtle, often hidden aspects of their team's experience. In this intuitive understanding, they create a culture of respect, a space where people feel seen, valued, and understood beyond their words.

Reflect on your own sense of empathy. Do you listen beyond what is said, or do you rely only on explicit communication? Leaders who embrace intuition develop a sense of empathy that transcends words, a way of connecting that goes beyond the obvious. They create environments where people feel safe to be themselves, where they do not need to spell out every need because they know their leader understands. This intuitive empathy is a quiet strength, a force that fosters loyalty and trust, a reminder that true leadership sees beyond appearances.

Intuition is also essential in moments of rapid decision-making. When time is limited, intuition becomes the guide that cuts through uncertainty, allowing leaders to act decisively. In the gorilla troop, the silverback's instincts guide him through moments of immediate danger, allowing him to respond without hesitation. He does not pause to deliberate; he trusts his instincts, acting with a swiftness and confidence that ensures the safety of the group. His decisions are not made in haste; they are guided by a deep trust in his own awareness, his own understanding.

As leaders, this intuitive decisiveness is invaluable. In times of crisis, intuition becomes the force that allows us to act with confidence, to move forward without second-guessing. Leaders who trust their instincts in these moments project a strength that others can rely upon, a resilience that is unshaken by fear or doubt. This intuitive decisiveness is not rash; it is the product of a cultivated awareness, a trust that has been built over time. In intuition, we find the courage to act when others hesitate, the strength to lead even in the face of uncertainty.

Consider your own approach to rapid decision-making. Do you trust your instincts, or do you become caught in analysis, in hesitation? Leaders who honor their intuition in these moments inspire confidence, creating a sense of direction that others can follow. Intuition becomes a guide, a force that allows us to act with clarity and purpose, a reminder that sometimes the best decisions come not from overthinking but from trusting our own inner knowing.

In leadership, intuition is also a source of innovation. The logical mind often moves within established boundaries, but intuition allows us to explore beyond them, to see possibilities that lie outside the conventional. The silverback, though rooted in instinct, adapts to new challenges with flexibility. His intuition guides him through unfamiliar situations, allowing him to respond creatively, to find solutions that logic alone might overlook. This intuitive adaptability is a source of strength, a reminder that true resilience lies not in rigid adherence to rules but in the freedom to explore new paths.

Reflect on your own approach to innovation. Do you allow intuition to guide you beyond the familiar, or do you stay within the boundaries of logic and predictability? Leaders who embrace

INSTINCTS AND INTUITION

intuition create a culture where creativity is valued, where new ideas are encouraged, where the unknown is not feared but welcomed. Intuition fosters a mindset of openness, a willingness to explore, to innovate, to move beyond what is known. In intuition, we find the courage to break free from convention, to lead not only with intelligence but with imagination.

Ultimately, instincts and intuition connect us to our own inner strength, a wisdom that is not taught but felt. In a world that often seeks certainty, intuition offers something more profound: a trust in ourselves, a faith in our own ability to navigate the unknown. To lead with intuition is to honor the wisdom within, to recognize that true strength comes not from external validation but from an inner confidence, a quiet knowing that does not waver in the face of doubt.

As you reflect on your own instincts, consider the value of intuition in your leadership. Do you listen to your inner voice, or do you rely solely on external measures of success? Leaders who honor their intuition create a foundation of self-trust, a strength that does not depend on the approval of others. In this self-trust, they find resilience, a grounded confidence that others can rely upon.

To lead like the silverback is to trust in the power of instinct and intuition, to understand that true wisdom is not always seen but felt, that true strength lies in a deep connection to oneself. This is the value of intuition. This is the essence of a truly insightful and resilient leader.

CHAPTER 18:

SIMPLE PLEASURES

Enjoy the little things, for one day you may look back and realize they were the big things
—Robert Brault

SIMPLE PLEASURES

Amid the grand pursuits, ambitions, and responsibilities of life, there exists a quiet yet profound truth: it is often the simplest pleasures that bring the greatest fulfillment. In leadership, and in life itself, there is a temptation to seek meaning only in monumental achievements, to view small moments as inconsequential, distractions from "bigger" things. Yet true wisdom recognizes that the beauty of life often lies in the ordinary, in the moments of calm, in the pleasures that require nothing but presence and appreciation. Simple pleasures are not a retreat from purpose; they are a reminder of it. They ground us, refresh us, and connect us to a sense of wholeness that transcends accomplishment.

Within a gorilla troop, simple pleasures are woven into the fabric of daily life. The gorillas find joy in grooming each other, in playing under the sun, in resting side by side in quiet companionship. These moments are not mere interruptions from their survival but essential parts of it. The troop does not live only in pursuit of food or safety; they live through these simple connections, these expressions of togetherness and contentment. Even the silverback, with his responsibilities and watchful vigilance, takes time to sit, to enjoy the warmth of the sun, to engage in playful moments with the young. These moments of simplicity are not distractions but affirmations of life itself.

As leaders, we must learn to honor the value of simple pleasures, to recognize that fulfillment is not found only in milestones but in moments. Simple pleasures are reminders that we are more than our achievements, that our lives are enriched not just by what we accomplish but by how deeply we connect to each moment. Leaders who embrace simplicity cultivate an environment where people feel free to experience joy, where purpose is not confined to productivity but includes the richness of human experience. In these small moments, there is a strength, a resilience that is not built on effort but on appreciation, on the willingness to be fully present.

Reflect on your own experience of simple pleasures. Do you allow yourself to enjoy these moments, or do you rush past them, seeing them as distractions? Leaders who embrace simplicity understand that there is power in presence, in the ability to be fully engaged with life as it unfolds. Simple pleasures ground us; they provide a space of refreshment, a reminder of the beauty that lies in the ordinary. When we learn to savor these moments, we create a foundation of contentment that sustains us, a strength that does not require constant achievement to feel whole.

In a gorilla troop, simple pleasures also serve to strengthen bonds. Grooming, playing, and resting together are expressions of connection, gestures that communicate care and belonging. These moments build trust, reinforcing the unity of the group without words. The silverback's participation in these moments is a reminder that even the strongest among them values connection, that leadership is not only about protection but about presence. As leaders, we must recognize the importance of these small acts, of the simple pleasures that foster connection and trust. When we take time to enjoy these moments with others, we create bonds that transcend hierarchy, bonds that are grounded in mutual respect and joy.

Consider the relationships within your team. Are they built only on goals and tasks, or do they include moments of genuine connection, of shared joy? Leaders who value simplicity create a culture where people feel seen not only for their roles but for who they are. They show that leadership is not just about achieving but about connecting, about creating spaces where people feel valued beyond their productivity. Simple pleasures create a sense of unity, a reminder that we are part of something larger, a community bound not only by purpose but by shared experiences of joy.

Simple pleasures also foster resilience. In times of stress or hardship, it is often these small moments that offer comfort, that remind us of the goodness in life despite its challenges. In the gorilla troop, even in times of scarcity or danger, moments of play, rest, and connection persist. They serve as a source of strength, a grounding force that brings the troop together, that provides a sense of continuity and peace. The silverback's calm presence in these moments reassures the group, showing them that even in difficulty, there is room for joy, for peace, for connection.

As leaders, embracing simple pleasures during challenging times requires strength. It is easy to fall into a cycle of stress, to lose ourselves in the demands of the moment. Yet the resilience found in simplicity offers a different path—a way to face difficulty without losing sight of joy. Leaders who embrace simplicity create an environment where people feel encouraged to find balance, to appreciate life's small moments even amid pressure. This resilience, this ability to find peace in simplicity, builds a foundation of strength that sustains through adversity.

Reflect on your response to hardship. Do you lose sight of simple pleasures, or do you allow them to ground you, to remind you of the beauty that remains? Leaders who value simplicity recognize that even in struggle, there are moments of grace, of connection, of joy. They create spaces where people feel supported, where resilience is built not through force but through appreciation, where each person feels empowered to find comfort in the small things that make life meaningful.

Simple pleasures also teach us to slow down, to resist the urge for constant progress. In a gorilla troop, life follows a natural rhythm. The gorillas are not constantly moving, constantly striving; they take time to rest, to enjoy each other's presence, to engage with their surroundings fully. The silverback does not push the troop to always be on guard; he allows moments of stillness, of ease. In these moments, there is a balance, a recognition that life is not only about survival but about experiencing it fully. As leaders, this rhythm is a powerful lesson. When we embrace the value of simple pleasures, we create a space where people feel free to breathe, to live without constant pressure.

Consider the pace of your own leadership. Do you allow moments of ease, or do you drive yourself and others forward without pause? Leaders who value simplicity create a culture where balance is respected, where people feel encouraged to find joy in the journey, not only in the destination. Simple pleasures slow us down, reminding us that life is not a race but a rhythm, a series of moments meant to be lived deeply, fully. In this slowing down, we find a strength that is grounded, a resilience that comes not from pushing forward but from connecting with the present.

In the end, simple pleasures connect us to our own humanity. They remind us that beyond roles, titles, and achievements, we are individuals with the capacity to experience life deeply. In a gorilla troop, these moments of simplicity bring each member back to themselves, to a sense of peace and belonging. The silverback's presence in these moments is a reminder that strength does not always require action; sometimes, it requires presence. Leaders who embrace simple pleasures lead not by force but by example, showing that life's meaning is found not only in what we accomplish but in how we experience each moment.

Reflect on the meaning you find in life's simple pleasures. Do you allow yourself to enjoy them fully, or do you view them as secondary to your responsibilities? Leaders who honor simplicity create a culture where people feel free to connect, to experience joy, to find meaning in small acts. They lead by showing that strength is not found in constant striving but in the ability to appreciate life as it unfolds, in the willingness to find contentment in what is here, now.

Simple pleasures also remind us of gratitude. In the rush to achieve, it is easy to forget the beauty of what we already have. But when we embrace simplicity, we reconnect with a sense of gratitude, a recognition of the gifts that surround us. The gorilla troop, in their moments of play, of grooming, of quiet companionship, live with an unspoken gratitude for each other, for the warmth of the sun, for the abundance of the forest. The silverback's calm presence embodies this gratitude, a reminder that even with responsibilities, there is always room to appreciate.

Consider your own sense of gratitude. Do you recognize the gifts within each moment, or do you focus only on what is next, on what must be done? Leaders who value simplicity cultivate gratitude, creating environments where people feel encouraged to appreciate, to connect, to find fulfillment in the present. Gratitude is not a passive feeling; it is an active choice, a decision to honor the beauty of what is. In this gratitude, we find strength, a resilience that is rooted not in the pursuit of more but in the appreciation of what already is.

In the end, simple pleasures are not mere distractions; they are the essence of a life well-lived. They remind us that strength does not lie in constant striving but in the ability to find joy, peace, and fulfillment in each moment. To lead with simplicity is to create a community where people feel encouraged to live fully, to experience deeply, to find meaning in the small, quiet moments that make life rich.

To lead like the silverback is to understand the value of simple pleasures, to recognize that true strength lies not in grand pursuits alone but in the joy of life itself. This is the power of simplicity. This is the essence of a truly resilient and fulfilled life.

CHAPTER 19:

EATING TOGETHER

What I say is that, if a man really likes potatoes, he must be a pretty decent sort of fellow —A.A. Milne

There is something powerful, almost sacred, about the act of eating together. Across time and cultures, the shared meal has symbolized unity, an invitation to belong, and a ritual that brings people together in a way few other activities can. It is a time not just to nourish the body but to nurture connection, trust, and companionship. Leaders who recognize the importance of communal meals understand that eating together is not simply a way to satisfy hunger; it is a way to build community, to create bonds that go beyond the surface, to reinforce the unity that underpins collective strength.

In a gorilla troop, eating together is part of the daily rhythm. Though they forage separately, the gorillas often gather to eat close by, a shared ritual that connects them in their most basic needs. This gathering is not forced; it is instinctive. By eating near each other, they reinforce bonds, communicate a sense of safety, and enjoy a mutual presence that goes beyond mere survival. The silverback, though the leader, eats alongside the troop, displaying an equality that is rarely seen in other moments. Eating together here is an expression of trust, a grounding force that brings the troop together in a shared, peaceful purpose.

As leaders, understanding the value of eating together requires us to look beyond productivity and efficiency. Shared meals are not interruptions; they are investments. They create an atmosphere where people feel comfortable, where hierarchies soften, and where individuals can connect on a human level. Leaders who embrace the ritual of eating together cultivate an environment where people feel valued not only for what they do but for who they are. This unity builds a foundation of trust, a reminder that we are all part of the same team, that in our shared humanity lies our collective strength.

Reflect on your own experiences of eating with others. Are they moments of connection, or do they feel like hurried necessities, lost in the rush of daily tasks? Leaders who understand the importance of shared meals approach them with intention, viewing each shared meal as an opportunity to strengthen the team, to create a sense of belonging. In these moments, there is a grounding force, a sense of unity that is not built on words or roles but on shared experience. Eating together reminds us that, beyond our roles and responsibilities, we share a fundamental connection.

In a gorilla troop, eating together also serves as a way to reinforce trust. The silverback, though powerful, does not separate himself from the troop during meals. His presence among them as they eat is a silent statement: We are safe here; we are together. His role as protector is subtly communicated without action, just by being there. This shared meal creates a sense of security, a reminder that they can relax, eat, and enjoy the company of the troop. For leaders, this is a powerful reminder. By participating in shared meals, leaders communicate solidarity, a sense that they are part of the team, not separate from it.

Consider the impact of your own presence during meals with your team. Do you engage in these shared moments, or do you separate yourself, overlooking the opportunity for connection? Leaders who eat with their teams build a unique form of trust, a bond that goes beyond professional roles. In eating together, they communicate that they are not only leaders but equals, part of the same shared purpose. This trust is not built through words but through shared ritual, through the simple yet profound act of breaking bread together.

Eating together also fosters open communication. In the structured environment of meetings or discussions, conversation is often guided by objectives, agendas, and outcomes. But at the table, conversation flows more freely, barriers soften, and people feel safe to express themselves openly. In the gorilla troop, mealtimes are times of ease, moments when the tensions of daily survival lessen, and the group can relax. The young play nearby, the mothers rest, and the silverback observes in peace. This atmosphere of ease creates a space for natural interaction, a place where individuals can feel fully present without the constraints of formality.

As leaders, we can learn from this natural ease. By creating an environment where people feel free to connect over meals, leaders foster open communication, a culture where people feel safe to share ideas, thoughts, and perspectives without fear of judgment. These shared meals create a bridge, a space where conversations flow from a place of authenticity rather than agenda. In this freedom, there is an honesty that builds trust, a sense that each voice matters. Leaders who embrace these moments create a culture of openness, an environment where people feel valued not only for their contributions but for who they are.

Reflect on the communication within your own team. Do you allow space for open, unstructured conversation, or is every interaction defined by purpose and efficiency? Leaders who value shared meals recognize that some of the most valuable conversations happen outside of formal settings. They understand that eating together creates a space where people feel free to speak, to connect, to share. This openness is the foundation of true connection, a reminder that genuine communication is not forced but emerges naturally in moments of shared presence.

Eating together also reinforces a sense of gratitude. In the gorilla troop, food is never taken for granted. The daily search for nourishment is a reminder of life's fragility, of the dependence each member has on the environment, on the group. When they gather to eat, it is a shared experience of survival, a silent acknowledgment of gratitude for the food that sustains them. This act of eating together, then, becomes a ritual of appreciation, a moment of unity that goes beyond the physical act of eating to encompass a shared acknowledgment of life's gifts.

As leaders, embracing this sense of gratitude within shared meals deepens our connection to those we lead. By viewing meals as moments of appreciation, we communicate that we do not take these shared moments for granted, that we value each person's presence and contribution. Leaders who bring gratitude to the table create an atmosphere of respect, a sense that each person's presence is valued. In this gratitude, there is a humility that strengthens the group, a reminder that each person, regardless of role, is essential to the whole.

Reflect on your own sense of gratitude within shared meals. Do you view them as opportunities for connection, or do you treat them as routine? Leaders who approach meals with gratitude create an environment where people feel respected, where the act of eating together becomes more than sustenance. It becomes a moment of shared appreciation, a reminder that each person contributes to the whole, that in their togetherness, there is strength.

In leadership, eating together also serves as a means of grounding. In a world that often prioritizes speed and productivity, meals offer a moment of pause, a reminder that life is not only about doing but about being. The gorilla troop does not rush through meals; they savor them, taking time to enjoy the nourishment, the company, the peace. The silverback, though vigilant, participates in this rhythm, allowing himself and the troop to simply exist in the moment. As leaders, this grounding is essential. By eating together, we create a space where people feel free to slow down, to engage fully, to enjoy the present without the pressure of constant movement.

Consider the pace of your own leadership. Do you allow moments for grounding, or are meals treated as interruptions to productivity? Leaders who embrace the ritual of eating together create an atmosphere where people feel encouraged to pause, to connect, to find strength in simply being together. This grounding brings a sense of balance, a reminder that life's value is found not only in what we accomplish but in how we experience it, in the shared moments that bring us back to ourselves and to each other.

In the end, eating together is more than a shared meal; it is a ritual of unity, a reminder that we are all connected by our most basic needs, that beyond roles and titles, we are human. To lead with this understanding is to create a community where people feel seen, valued, and connected. Eating together is an act of trust, a moment of presence, a source of strength that transcends the physical and reaches into the heart of community.

To lead like the silverback is to recognize the value of eating together, to understand that true leadership is not only about directing but about connecting, about creating spaces where people feel a sense of belonging, a sense of shared purpose. This is the power of eating together. This is the essence of a truly united and resilient community.

CHAPTER 20:

TAKING TIME TO REST

❝❞

Almost everything will work again if you unplug it for a few minutes, including you
—Anne Lamott

TAKING TIME TO REST

In a world that glorifies constant movement and endless productivity, the value of rest is often forgotten. We are taught to pursue, to strive, to keep pushing forward, as though stillness were a waste of potential. Yet, true wisdom recognizes that rest is not only necessary; it is essential. Rest is not an interruption in our purpose, but a vital part of it. To lead well, to live fully, one must learn the art of pausing, of stepping back to gather strength, to renew perspective. Rest is not a retreat from life; it is a return to it, a moment to reconnect with ourselves, our purpose, and our inner strength.

In the natural rhythm of a gorilla troop, rest is a deeply respected part of life. The gorillas do not view rest as an afterthought; they see it as a time of unity, recovery, and peace. Throughout the day, the troop moves with intention, yet they know when to pause, when to sit quietly, when to lie side by side in tranquil companionship. Even the silverback, with all his responsibilities, understands the need to rest, to let go of vigilance for a moment and allow himself to simply be. This balance between action and rest is what sustains the troop, what keeps them resilient, unified, and strong.

As leaders, embracing rest is a radical act in a world that worships constant progress. To rest is to say, "I value my strength too much to spend it recklessly." It is to understand that growth is not only found in action but in reflection, in moments of quiet renewal. Leaders who embrace rest create an environment where people feel free to pause, to rejuvenate, to find their own rhythm. They understand that strength is not sustained by continuous effort, but by the willingness to step back, to breathe, to allow the mind and body the space to recover fully.

Reflect on your own approach to rest. Do you view it as a necessary part of life, or do you treat it as an inconvenience, something to squeeze in when everything else is done? Leaders who value rest understand that it is not merely recovery but renewal, a time to reconnect with the essence of who we are, to replenish the well from which we draw our strength. Rest is an act of respect—for ourselves, for our purpose, and for those we lead. In rest, we find the foundation of resilience, a strength that endures because it is cared for.

In a gorilla troop, rest also serves as a time of unity. When they lie together, side by side, they are not simply sleeping; they are reaffirming their bonds, grounding themselves in the presence of each other. The silverback, though he remains the leader, becomes simply part of the group in these moments, a reminder that rest transcends roles. It is a shared experience, a ritual that binds the troop in quiet solidarity. For leaders, this is a powerful lesson. Rest is not merely an individual need but a communal one. By encouraging rest within a team, leaders create a culture where people feel free to recharge, where unity is reinforced not through constant activity but through shared moments of calm.

Consider the atmosphere within your own team. Do you encourage rest, or is the focus always on movement, on productivity? Leaders who value rest foster a culture of balance, creating a space where people feel empowered to find their own rhythm. In this encouragement, there is respect, a recognition that each person's strength is important, that their well-being matters. Rest is a reminder that we are not machines, that our value is not measured by constant output but by our presence, our resilience, our capacity to lead and live well.

Taking time to rest also cultivates clarity. In the noise of constant activity, clarity is easily lost, drowned out by the demands of the moment. But in stillness, in rest, the mind finds its center, the heart reconnects with its purpose. In the gorilla troop, rest allows each member to simply exist, to let go of the demands of the day, to find peace in the simplicity of presence. The silverback, in his moments of quiet, is not only resting his body but centering his mind, reconnecting with his role, his responsibility, his purpose. This clarity, this alignment, is what gives his leadership depth and stability.

As leaders, clarity is a rare and precious resource. It is easy to lose sight of purpose in the rush of tasks and expectations. Rest, then, is an opportunity—a time to reflect, to realign, to rediscover the reason behind the action. Leaders who embrace rest gain perspective, a broader view that allows them to see beyond the immediate. They act not from urgency but from intention, guided by a clear understanding of what truly matters. In rest, we find the wisdom to lead not from reaction but from purpose.

Reflect on your own clarity. Do you take time to reconnect with your purpose, or do you allow yourself to be pulled in all directions?

Leaders who value rest understand that clarity is not found in constant movement but in moments of quiet, in the willingness to step back and see the bigger picture. In rest, we find a calmness that guides us, a perspective that enables us to make decisions grounded in truth, not in pressure.

In leadership, rest also fosters creativity. The mind, when constantly engaged, can become rigid, focused only on what must be done. But in rest, the mind is free to wander, to explore, to dream. The silverback, though powerful, does not spend every moment in vigilance. He allows himself time to sit, to observe, to simply exist. In these moments, his awareness deepens, his understanding of his environment expands. For leaders, rest is a source of creativity, a space where ideas emerge, where solutions are found not through effort but through openness, through the willingness to let the mind breathe.

Consider your approach to creativity. Do you give yourself time to rest, to allow ideas to emerge naturally, or do you force solutions through continuous effort? Leaders who embrace rest understand that creativity is not born from pressure but from freedom. They create a culture where people feel encouraged to take breaks, to step back, to let inspiration find them. In rest, we find a creativity that is not forced but flows naturally, a reminder that some of the best ideas come not from relentless pursuit but from the quiet moments in between.

Rest is also a profound act of humility. In a world that values endless productivity, taking time to rest can feel like a surrender, an admission that we are not limitless. Yet, there is strength in this humility, a recognition that we are human, that our value is not measured by how much we can endure but by how well we care for ourselves. The silverback, though strong, does not deny his need for rest. He rests openly, without shame, showing the troop that strength includes knowing when to pause. For leaders, this is a powerful example. Rest is not weakness; it is wisdom, a reminder that we are not invincible, that our resilience requires respect and care.

Reflect on your own relationship with humility. Do you view rest as a weakness, or do you see it as an act of respect for your own strength? Leaders who embrace rest show that they value their well-being, that they understand the limits of endurance. In this humility, there is a quiet strength, a resilience that does not push beyond reason but finds balance, a reminder that true power lies in knowing when to act and when to pause.

Rest also allows us to connect more deeply with ourselves. In the silence of rest, we come face to face with our own thoughts, our own fears, our own desires. The silverback, in his moments of solitude, is not only resting his body but connecting with his own instincts, his own wisdom. This inner connection is the foundation of his strength, a depth of self-awareness that guides him in his role. Leaders who take time to rest cultivate this same self-connection, a strength that is grounded not in external validation but in a deep relationship with themselves.

Consider your own self-awareness. Do you give yourself time to connect with your own thoughts, to understand your own needs, or do you lose yourself in the demands of others? Leaders who embrace rest cultivate a relationship with themselves, a foundation of self-knowledge that guides their actions. In rest, they find a strength that is unshakable, a resilience that comes from within, a reminder that true leadership begins with self-mastery.

In the end, taking time to rest is not an indulgence; it is a necessity, a foundation upon which true strength is built. To lead well, to live fully, one must honor the rhythm of rest, the balance that sustains life. Rest is not a retreat from purpose but a return to it, a reminder that our value lies not in constant action but in our presence, our clarity, our ability to live and lead with intention.

To lead like the silverback is to understand the value of rest, to know that true strength lies not in relentless pursuit but in the balance of action and stillness, in the willingness to pause, to renew, to reconnect with oneself and with the world. This is the power of rest. This is the essence of a truly resilient and fulfilled life.

CONCLUSION

As we reach the end of this journey, it's time to pause and reflect on the path that has led us here. Through each chapter, we've explored the wisdom embedded in gorilla life—the strength, resilience, and quiet power that emanate from their way of being. We've delved into the lessons that come from observing the silverback's leadership, his ability to create harmony within the troop, to balance protection with compassion, presence with rest, and action with stillness. These qualities remind us that true leadership is neither a title nor a set of skills alone; it is a way of life, a reflection of our values, our presence, and our commitment to the people and communities we serve.

In a world that is often driven by urgency, competition, and relentless progress, Live and Lead Like a Gorilla offers a different vision—a vision that invites us to lead with calm confidence, with trust in our instincts, and with the understanding that our power lies not in controlling others but in knowing ourselves. Gorillas show us that strength is not a performance; it is a quiet confidence that does not need to announce itself. By embracing this model of leadership, we open ourselves to a life that is not only effective but fulfilling, not only strong but deeply meaningful.

Returning to the Basics

At the heart of this book is a return to simplicity. The gorilla troop thrives by honoring the fundamentals: connection, rest, protection, and presence. These are the cornerstones of authentic leadership, reminders that complexity is not a substitute for wisdom. By rooting ourselves in these essentials, we strip away the noise and distractions that often cloud our purpose. We are left with the clarity that leadership is not about endless striving but about creating an environment of safety, trust, and unity.

This simplicity is not a retreat from life's challenges but a foundation upon which to face them. As you move forward from this book, remember that the strength of a leader does not come from outward displays or constant busyness, but from the quiet discipline of living one's values, of building relationships based on respect and empathy. True leadership is found in the ability to create spaces where others feel seen, valued, and encouraged to grow. This simplicity is a powerful guide—one that leads us back to the fundamentals of what it means to lead and to live with integrity.

Embracing the Rhythm of Leadership

The gorilla troop lives in harmony with natural rhythms, understanding that life is not a straight line but a cycle of effort and rest, action and reflection. Leadership, too, is a rhythm—a balance between pushing forward and knowing when to pause. The silverback's strength is rooted in his understanding of this rhythm; he knows when to act, when to stand back, and when to simply be present. This rhythm, this ebb and flow, is what sustains him and his troop.

As leaders, embracing this rhythm allows us to avoid burnout, to lead with consistency rather than bursts of energy that quickly fade. When we honor the need for rest, when we give ourselves time to reflect, we become stronger, more grounded, and better able to respond to life's demands. In leading others, we set the tone, modeling resilience not through relentless pursuit but through respect for balance. This rhythm is a reminder that leadership is not about driving endlessly forward but about creating a sustainable path that respects both our own needs and those of the people we lead.

Cultivating Connection and Trust

The gorilla troop thrives on connection, on a trust that is built through presence and shared experience. The silverback does not command loyalty through force; he earns it through consistent, quiet authority and a deep commitment to the welfare of his troop. He leads by creating an environment of trust, a place where each member feels safe to be themselves, to find their own strengths within the collective support of the group.

As leaders, the ability to cultivate this connection and trust is invaluable. In a society that often prizes individual achievement, the lesson of the gorilla troop reminds us that our true strength lies in unity, in a trust that cannot be forced but must be earned. Leadership is not about coercion; it is about creating a community where people feel a sense of belonging, where their contributions are valued, and where they can grow. In the end, this connection is the greatest measure of our leadership—the relationships we build, the trust we foster, and the impact we leave on the lives of others.

The Courage to Rest and Reflect

In the final chapter, we explored the essential nature of rest, a reminder that even the strongest among us require time to recharge, to reconnect with our purpose, and to renew our energy. The gorilla troop, with its natural rhythms, shows us that rest is not a luxury but a necessity, a foundation of resilience. The silverback does not spend every moment on guard; he knows the value of quiet, of stillness, of recovery. This wisdom is vital for us as leaders.

As you move forward, remember that rest is an act of courage, a commitment to sustainable strength. In a culture that often views rest as weakness, the decision to pause, to breathe, to gather oneself is a revolutionary act. It is a declaration that we value our well-being, that we understand the limits of our strength, and that we are committed to leading from a place of fullness rather than depletion. Rest is where we find clarity, where we reconnect with our deepest intentions, where we cultivate the patience to lead well.

An Invitation to Lead Authentically

Live and Lead Like a Gorilla is, above all, an invitation to authenticity. It calls us to strip away the superficial trappings of leadership and to embrace a model that is grounded, compassionate, and true. This book does not offer a formula for success but a path to fulfillment—a way to lead that aligns with our values, respects the humanity of those around us, and builds a legacy that endures. Leadership, when done well, is not about achieving titles or accolades; it is about living in a way that elevates those we lead, creating a space where others feel empowered to realize their own potential.

The journey does not end with this book. Each chapter has offered insights, but it is up to you to bring them to life, to integrate them into your own path. Remember that leadership is not something to be perfected; it is something to be practiced, explored, refined. The silverback does not lead perfectly, but he leads with presence, with integrity, with an unwavering commitment to his troop. As you step forward, allow yourself to be imperfect, to grow, to learn from each experience. This is the essence of authentic leadership—a willingness to show up fully, to lead from the heart, to honor each moment as an opportunity to live and lead with intention.

A Legacy of Strength and Compassion

In the end, Live and Lead Like a Gorilla is about leaving a legacy—a legacy of strength that is balanced with compassion, of resilience that is softened by empathy, of purpose that is grounded in presence. Just as the silverback's influence extends beyond his lifetime, shaping the lives of those he has led, your leadership has the potential to leave a lasting impact. Each choice you make, each interaction, each moment of connection contributes to the legacy you leave.

May this journey inspire you to lead with courage, to live with intention, and to embrace the strength within yourself. Leadership is not a destination; it is a journey, one that calls for constant growth, reflection, and renewal. Like the gorillas in their natural rhythms, may you find your own balance, your own wisdom, and your own strength in both the quiet and the active moments.

Thank you for joining this journey. As you go forth, remember that true leadership is not about the positions you hold or the power you wield. It is about the lives you touch, the trust you build, and the authenticity with which you live. Live and lead with the quiet confidence of the silverback, with the calm strength that inspires, the presence that reassures, and the compassion that unites.

Welcome to the legacy of gorilla-inspired leadership. May it serve you well in every moment of your life and every act of your leadership.

ABOUT THE AUTHOR

Brian Edwards is a leader, entrepreneur, and mentor who has dedicated his life to cultivating resilience, compassion, and growth in those around him. Based in Raleigh, North Carolina, Brian's career journey spans diverse fields, from corporate leadership to entrepreneurship, all grounded in a philosophy that views leadership as an act of service, trust, and human connection. For over a decade, he has led teams as a store manager for a major home improvement chain, creating an atmosphere where people feel valued, empowered, and encouraged to grow.

Before transitioning to corporate leadership, Brian's entrepreneurial drive led him to found and operate a range of successful ventures. From Coastline Retail Services to Island Landscaping, Trademark Investments, Baseline Concrete, and even a popular restaurant called Los Primos, each business reflects his adaptability and resourcefulness. Across vastly different markets, Brian's ventures have thrived because he approaches each new challenge with a commitment to understanding people, honing his vision, and fostering authentic connections. His success across these ventures is rooted not only in keen business insight but in his capacity to see each venture as an opportunity to build community and uplift those he works with.

Brian's philosophy of leadership is defined by his belief that true leadership is not about enforcing structure or control but about cultivating potential. To him, each individual has unique strengths, and a leader's role is to create an environment where these strengths can flourish. He values loyalty, heart, and dedication over credentials, recognizing potential that goes beyond the surface. Success, to Brian, is not measured solely by results but by the growth, confidence, and sense of belonging he inspires in those he leads.

His passion for leadership extends beyond the workplace. As a mentor, he dedicates time to guiding young people, passing on lessons forged through both triumph and hardship. Through mentorship, Brian seeks to instill values of resilience, integrity, and hard work, laying a foundation that will guide his mentees throughout their lives. For Brian, mentorship is a way to give back, to support the next generation as they learn to lead with intention, empathy, and strength.

Outside of his leadership and mentorship roles, Brian is an avid day trader, applying the same strategic focus to financial markets that he brings to his businesses. His fascination with market trends reflects his passion for calculated decision-making and his dedication to continual growth and challenge.

ABOUT THE AUTHOR

Brian's journey has not been without profound trials. Once a Division I collegiate basketball player and MVP, he has faced life's highs and lows, including the unimaginable loss of his son, Ethan. In the wake of this tragedy, Brian turned to writing as a way to process his grief and find healing. Writing has since become an outlet for him to explore and share his perspectives on resilience, leadership, and personal growth. Through his words, he channels his experiences to uplift others, using his journey to inspire those facing their own challenges.

Today, Brian's dedication to leadership is stronger than ever, and his life experiences have only deepened his understanding of perseverance, compassion, and adaptability. In every role he takes on, Brian strives to embody the principles he believes define true leadership: lead with compassion, empower others, and prioritize people over processes. To Brian, leadership is a commitment to elevating those around him, a responsibility he embraces with humility, integrity, and heart.

Made in the USA
Columbia, SC
21 December 2024